THIS
BOOK
Belongs
To

Marion Deuchars

LET'S MAKE some GREAT ART

"Some painters transform the sun into a yellow spot, others transform a yellow spot into the sun."

Pablo Picasso

LAURENCE KING

PUBLISHED IN 2011 by

LAURENCE KING PUBLISHING Ltd
361 - 373 CITY ROAD
LONDON EC1V 1LR
Tel + 44 20 7841 6900
Fax + 44 20 7841 6910
www. laurenceking. com
enquiries@ laurenceking.com

Reprinted in 2011 (twice), 2012 (twice), 2013, 2014, 2015 (twice), 2016

A CATALOGUE RECORD OF THIS BOOK IS AVAILABLE FROM THE BRITISH LIBRARY.

ISBN 978-1-85669-7-866

Printed in China

FOR Hamish and Alexander
x

ART MATERIALS

A LIST OF BASIC
ART MATERIALS

WHITE GLUE (OR GLUE STICK)

SCISSORS

CONSTRUCTION PAPER
(in different sizes and colours)

RULER
PENCILS
COLOURED PENCILS
PENS
TAPE
PAINT BRUSHES (different sizes)
CRAYONS OR PASTELS

PAINTS
DRAWING COMPASS
ERASER
PENCIL SHARPENER
WATER CONTAINER
PALETTE.
INK

PENCILS

WATER SOLUBLE
This means when you add water
they change from pencil to
watercolour.

PENCILS
COME IN ALL
SHAPES AND
SIZES.
TRY TO HAVE
A DIFFERENT
RANGE, FROM
HARD TO SOFT.

CHALKS
AND
PASTELS

COME IN BEAUTIFUL COLOURS.

THEY HAVE A 'PAINTING-EFFECT'
WHEN YOU MIX OR BLEND THEM.

CHARCOAL IS
SOFT, BLACK AND
VELVET-LIKE TO
DRAW WITH.

GRAPHITE PENCIL OR STICK,
VERY GOOD FOR COVERING
LARGE AREAS ON THE PAPER.

ERASERS

REGULAR
ERASER
(HARD)

PUTTY
ERASER
(SOFT),
CAN BE
SQUEEZED
INTO SHAPES.

FELT-TIP PENS
COME IN ALL DIFFERENT
SHAPES AND SIZES. TRY
TO GET SOME THICK AND
THIN ONES.

BRUSH PENS
ARE USEFUL TOO. ↗

ROLLERS
ARE GREAT FOR
PAINTING LARGE
AREAS. OR USE ONE
TO MAKE YOUR OWN
COLOURED PAPER.

DRAWING
COMPASS

PAINTS

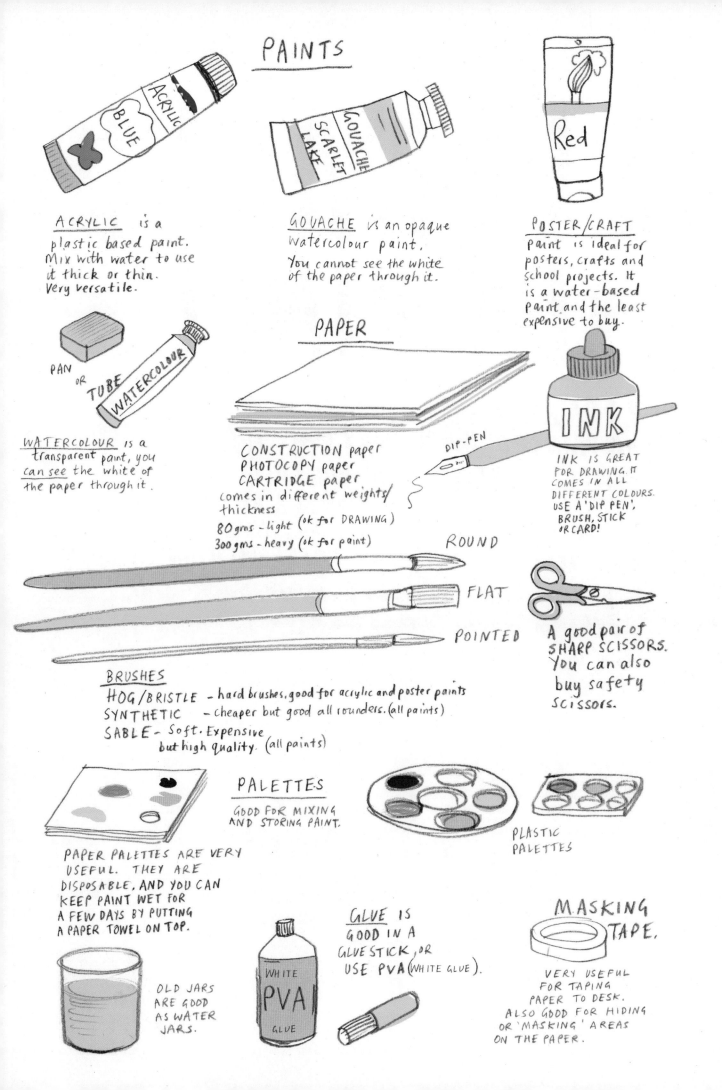

ACRYLIC is a plastic based paint. Mix with water to use it thick or thin. Very versatile.

GOUACHE is an opaque watercolour paint. You cannot see the white of the paper through it.

POSTER/CRAFT paint is ideal for posters, crafts and school projects. It is a water-based paint and the least expensive to buy.

PAN or TUBE WATERCOLOUR

WATERCOLOUR is a transparent paint, you can see the white of the paper through it.

PAPER

CONSTRUCTION paper
PHOTOCOPY paper
CARTRIDGE paper
comes in different weights/thickness
80 gms - light (ok for DRAWING)
300 gms - heavy (ok for paint)

DIP-PEN

INK

INK IS GREAT FOR DRAWING. IT COMES IN ALL DIFFERENT COLOURS. USE A 'DIP PEN', BRUSH, STICK OR CARD!

ROUND

FLAT

POINTED

BRUSHES
HOG/BRISTLE - hard brushes, good for acrylic and poster paints
SYNTHETIC - cheaper but good all rounders. (all paints)
SABLE - Soft. Expensive but high quality. (all paints)

A good pair of SHARP SCISSORS. You can also buy safety scissors.

PALETTES
GOOD FOR MIXING AND STORING PAINT.

PLASTIC PALETTES

PAPER PALETTES ARE VERY USEFUL. THEY ARE DISPOSABLE, AND YOU CAN KEEP PAINT WET FOR A FEW DAYS BY PUTTING A PAPER TOWEL ON TOP.

OLD JARS ARE GOOD AS WATER JARS.

WHITE PVA GLUE

GLUE IS GOOD IN A GLUE STICK, OR USE PVA (WHITE GLUE).

MASKING TAPE.

VERY USEFUL FOR TAPING PAPER TO DESK. ALSO GOOD FOR HIDING OR 'MASKING' AREAS ON THE PAPER.

LEONARDO DA VINCI

LEONARDO WAS BORN IN ITALY in 1452.
HE PAINTED 'The Mona Lisa'. THE MOST
FAMOUS PAINTING IN THE WORLD.
BUT, LEONARDO WAS NOT ONLY A PAINTER,
HE WAS A MUSICIAN, SCULPTOR, INVENTOR
ENGINEER, SCIENTIST and MATHEMATICIAN!

In his notebooks he used to write backwards,
so the only way to read his writing
was in a mirror.

can you
read this?
practice your
own mirror
writing.

Can you try to draw Mona Lisa's smile?

BASIC FORMS

BASIC FORMS ARE...

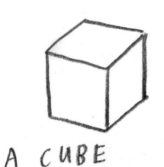

A CUBE

A CYLINDER

A SPHERE

TRY TO DRAW
THESE. ↘

IF YOU USE <u>SHADING</u>, THEY BECOME 3D

TRY TO DRAW
THESE. ↘

UPSIDE-DOWN DRAWING

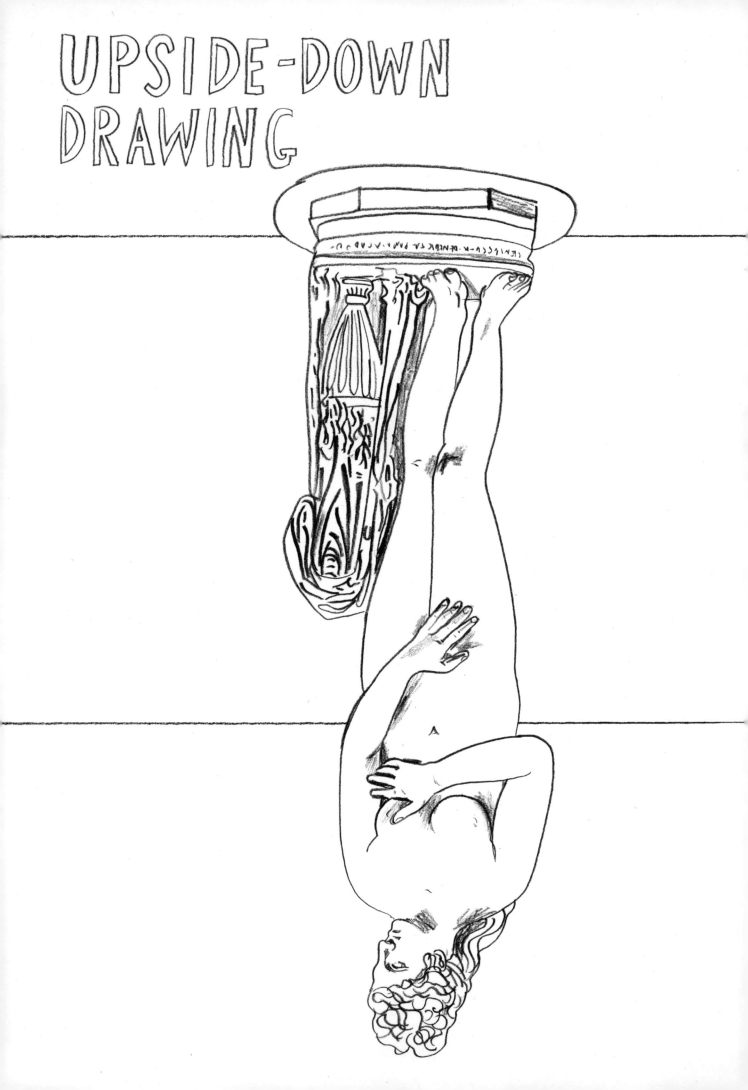

COPY THIS DRAWING.
DO NOT TURN THE DRAWING THE RIGHT WAY UP!
TRY TO DRAW IT WITHOUT THINKING WHAT IT IS.
JUST DRAW THE LINES AND SHAPES.
WHEN YOU FINISH, TURN YOUR DRAWING AROUND.

DARK TO LIGHT

PENCILS COME IN ALL DIFFERENT LEVELS OF HARDNESS. FROM VERY HARD TO VERY SOFT.

SOME ARE MARKED LIKE THIS:

(2H) VERY HARD

(H) MEDIUM HARD

(HB) WRITING/MEDIUM

(B) MEDIUM

(2B) MEDIUM SOFT

(4B) SOFT

(8B) VERY SOFT

PRACTICE HATCHING FROM DARK TO LIGHT.
IMAGINE YOUR HAND IS VERY HEAVY, THEN SLOWLY,
STROKE BY STROKE, IT GETS LIGHTER.

PRACTICE
GOING FROM DARK
TO LIGHT HERE.

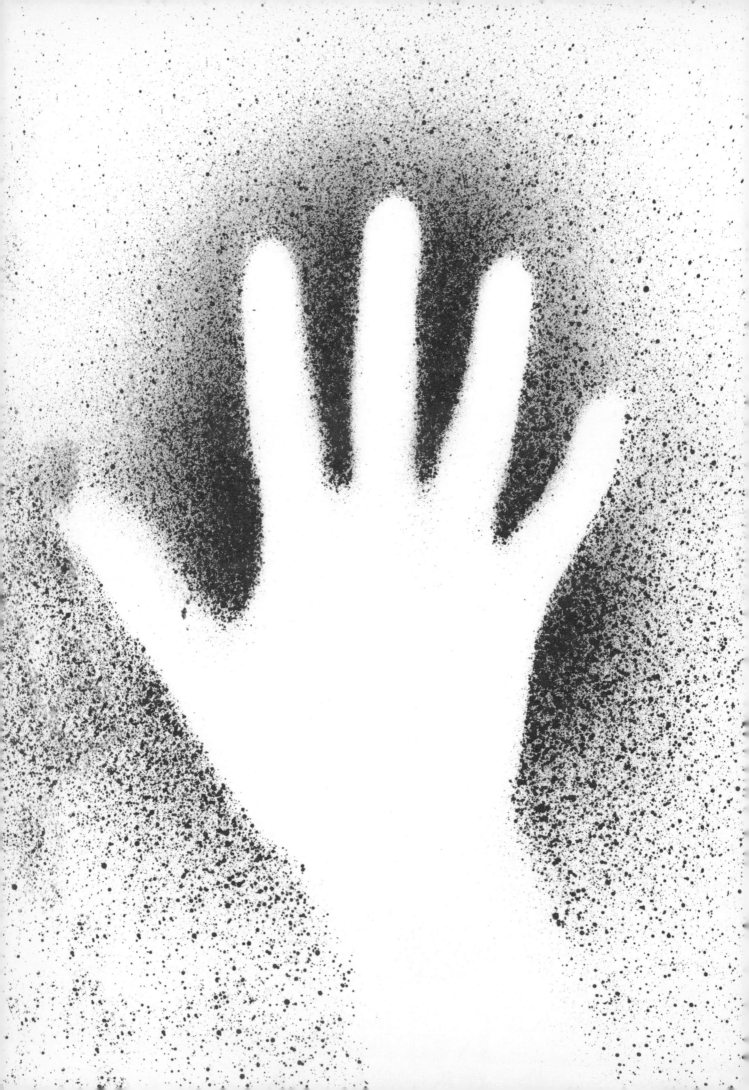

CAVE PAINTING

OVER 30,000 YEARS AGO, EARLY MAN MADE TRACINGS OF THEIR HANDS BY BLOWING PIGMENT THROUGH HOLLOW BONES OR DIRECTLY FROM THEIR MOUTHS.

USING AN OLD EMPTY BOTTLE WITH A SPRAY TOP, FILL WITH WATERY PAINT AND SPRAY YOUR HAND ON PAPER TO MAKE YOUR OWN CAVE ART.

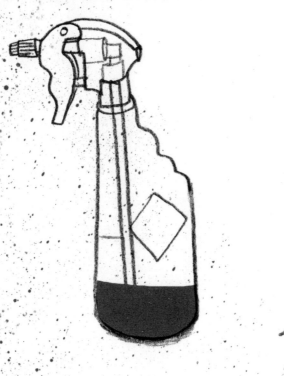

OR USE AN OLD TOOTHBRUSH!

THE MOST IMPORTANT THING IN DRAWING IS TO LOOK.

CURL YOUR HAND, NOW DRAW IT.
LOOK AT YOUR HAND MORE THAN THE PAPER.

USE **A TIMER**.
DRAW FOR 5 MINUTES.

NOW DRAW ANOTHER HAND FOR 30 SECONDS.

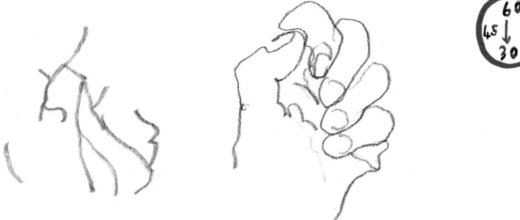

Attempt 1.

Attempt 2.

IN MY HOUSE, THERE ARE HOW MANY CHAIRS? ☐

CHOOSE TWO DIFFERENT ONES
PUT THEM NEXT TO, OR ON TOP
OF EACH OTHER, AND DRAW THEM.

IN MY HOUSE, THERE ARE HOW MANY PENCILS?

DRAW THEM.

↓

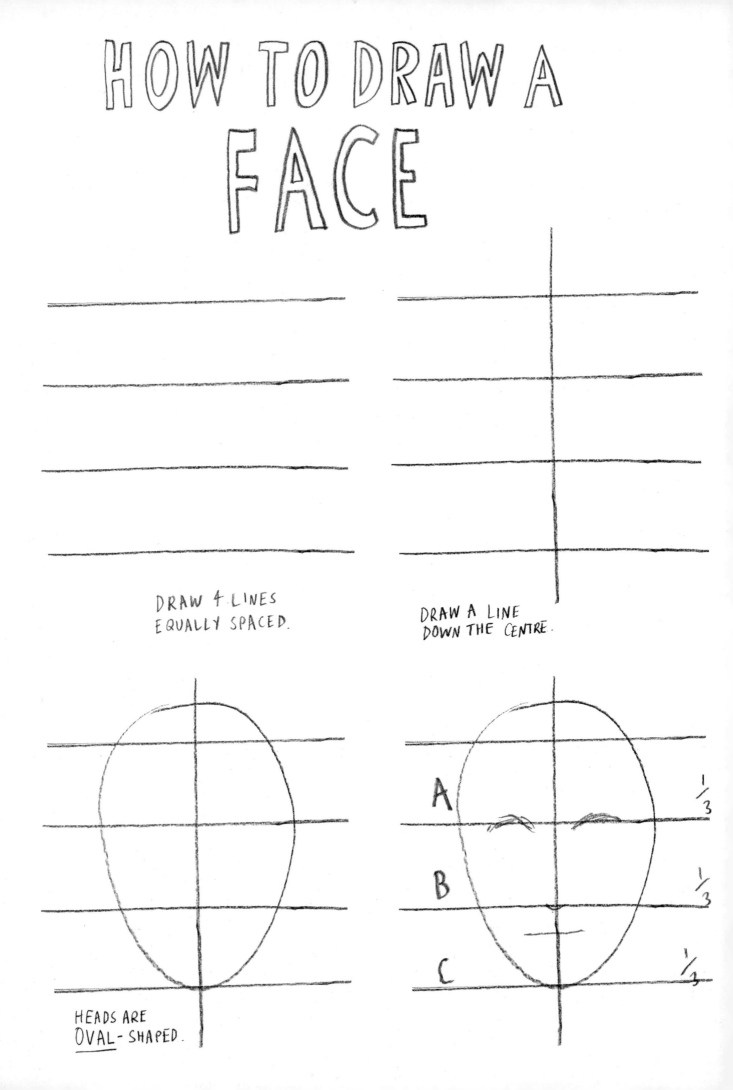

HOW TO DRAW A FACE

DRAW 4 LINES
EQUALLY SPACED.

DRAW A LINE
DOWN THE CENTRE.

HEADS ARE
OVAL-SHAPED.

A $\frac{1}{3}$

B $\frac{1}{3}$

C $\frac{1}{3}$

THE TOP OF THE
EARS ARE IN LINE
WITH THE TOP OF THE EYE.

THE SPACE BETWEEN
THE EYES IS ROUGHLY
THE SAME SIZE AS
AN EYE.

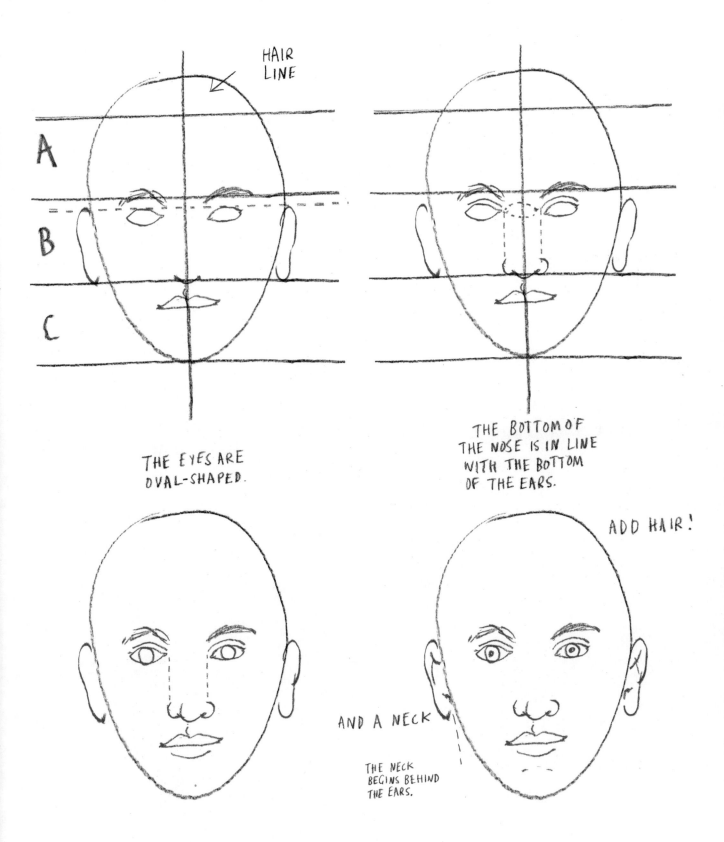

HAIR
LINE

A

B

C

THE EYES ARE
OVAL-SHAPED.

THE BOTTOM OF
THE NOSE IS IN LINE
WITH THE BOTTOM
OF THE EARS.

ADD HAIR!

AND A NECK

THE NECK
BEGINS BEHIND
THE EARS.

PABLO PICASSO

WAS BORN IN SPAIN IN 1881. HE IS FAMOUS FOR BEING THE CO-FOUNDER OF **CUBISM** WHICH

IS A STYLE OF PAINTING MADE UP OF CUBES, SPHERES, CYLINDERS, CONES AND OTHER GEOMETRIC SHAPES. THE PAINTINGS LOOK LIKE SOMEONE HAD CUT THEM UP AND GLUED THEM BACK TOGETHER!

MAKE A CUBIST STYLE PORTRAIT

DRAW OR PAINT YOUR FACE ON COLOURED PAPER. (OR COPY A PHOTOGRAPH OF A FACE).

CUT UP THE PICTURE INTO PIECES (NOT TOO SMALL).

STICK THE PIECES TO ANOTHER SHEET OF PAPER. TRY TO PUT THE PICTURE BACK TOGETHER IN A DIFFERENT ORDER TO MAKE A 'NEW FACE' FROM THE COMPONENTS.

AFRICAN

Some of Picasso's Art was influenced by African Art which helped create CUBISM.

FOLD A PIECE OF PAPER IN HALF AND PAINT HALF A FACE ON ONE SIDE. PRESS TOGETHER **WHILE** THE **PAINT** IS STILL WET. AND OPEN CAREFULLY.

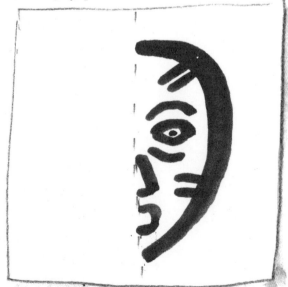

FOLD HERE ↻ AND PRESS

MASK

African Masks can
be made from wood,
bronze, copper, straw,
ceramic and textiles.
Many represent
animals and are
very colourful.

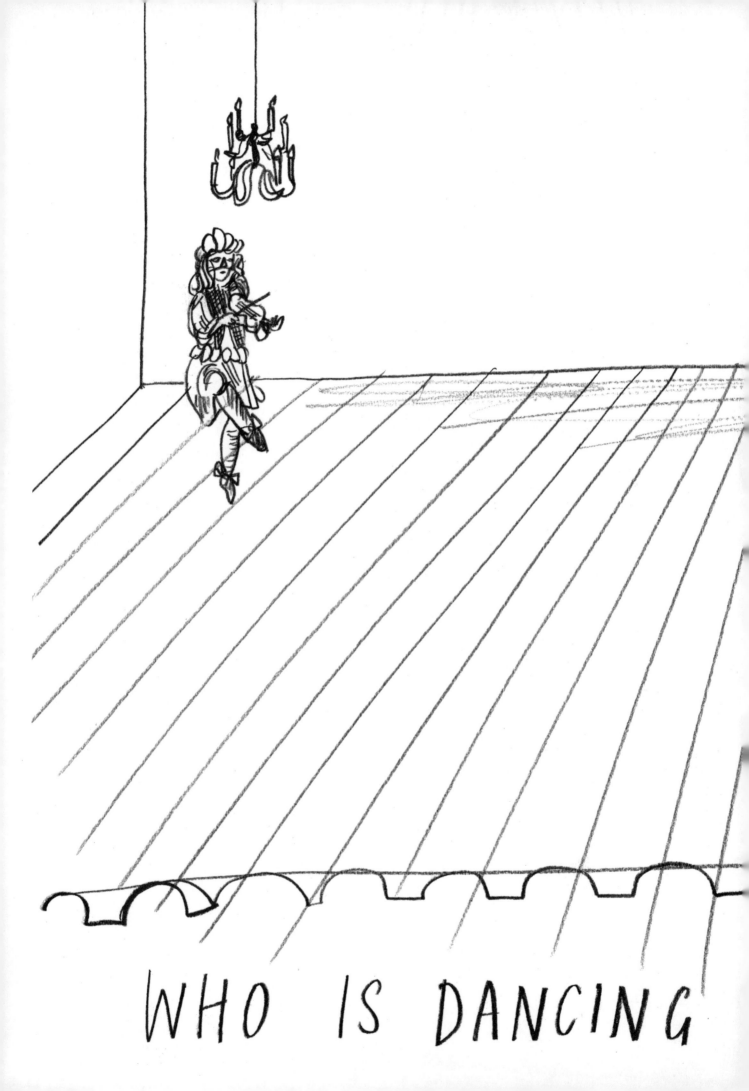

WHO IS DANCING

ON THE STAGE?

HOW TO DRAW A SIMPLE BIRD.

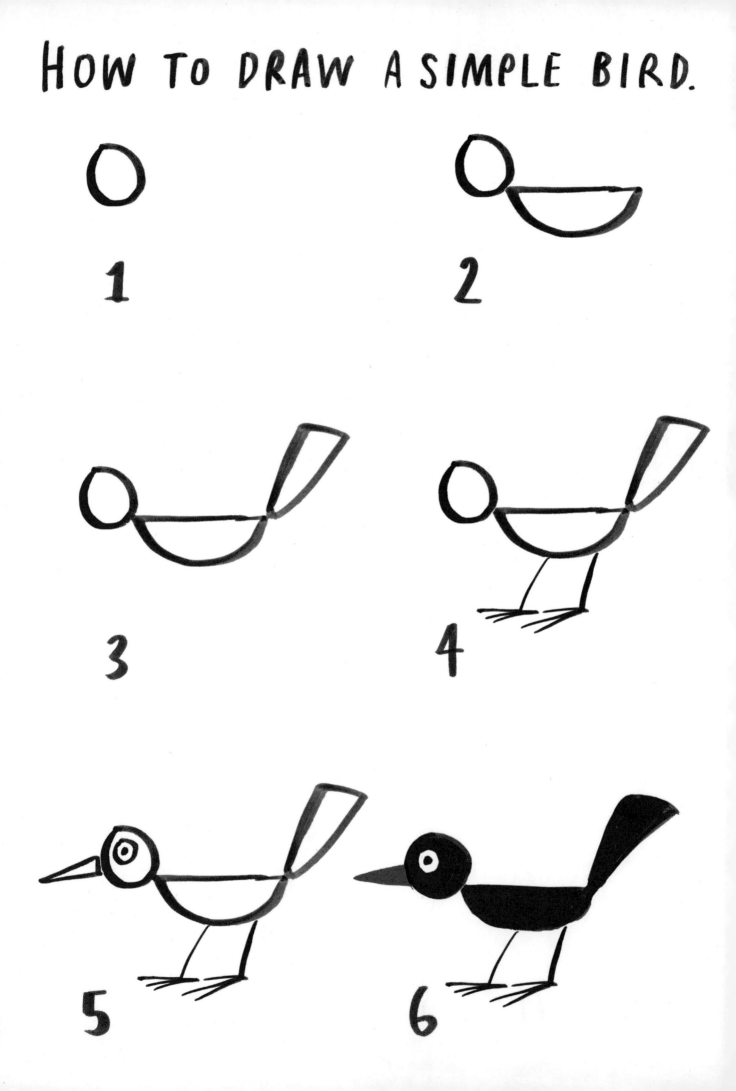

DRAW BIRDS HERE. ↙

1   2

3   4

5   6

DRAW BIRDS HERE.

↓

SURPRISED   SLEEPING

LOOKING UP   LOOKING DOWN

ANGRY   DEAD

SURPRISED

SLEEPING

LOOKING UP

LOOKING DOWN

ANGRY

DEAD

TAKE A PIECE OF PAPER. SIDE. - Before it dries: FOLD. FIRMLY. OPEN to see an

PUT SOME paint or Ink on ONE the PAPER in HALF and PRESS INK BLOT FACE or CREATURE.

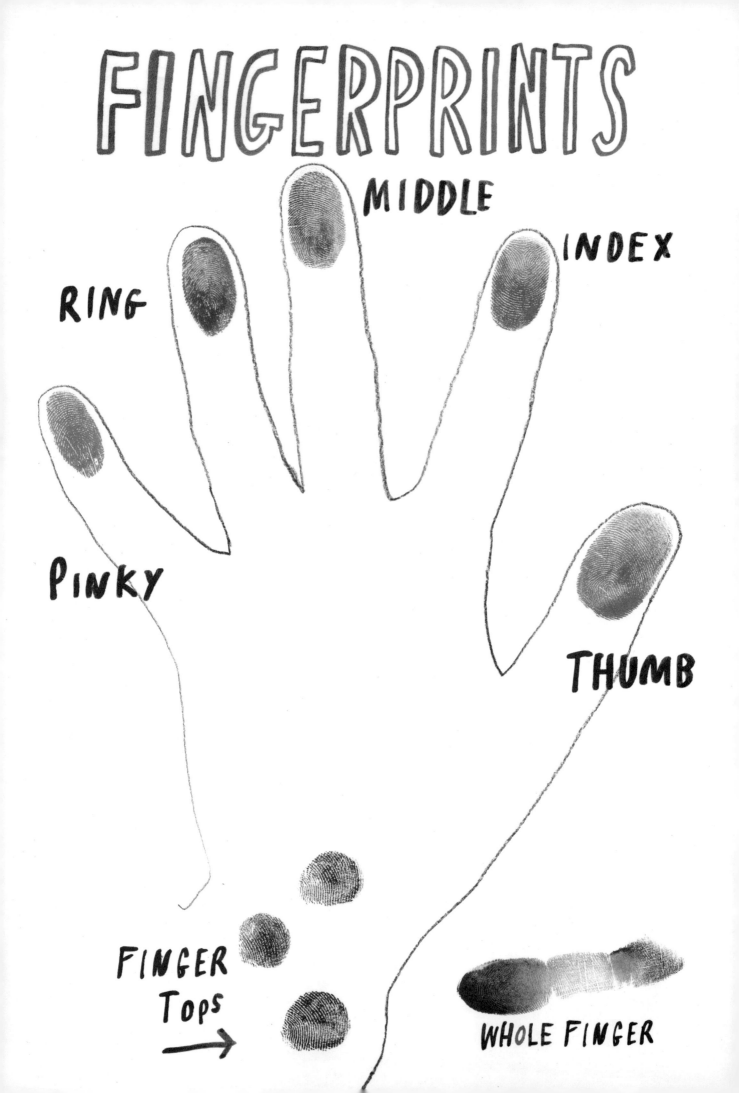

WHAT YOU NEED

INK PADS, PAPER, FINGERS!

Make stencils with bits of paper to make differently-shaped prints.

USE A PIECE OF PAPER OR CARD TO MAKE AN EDGE

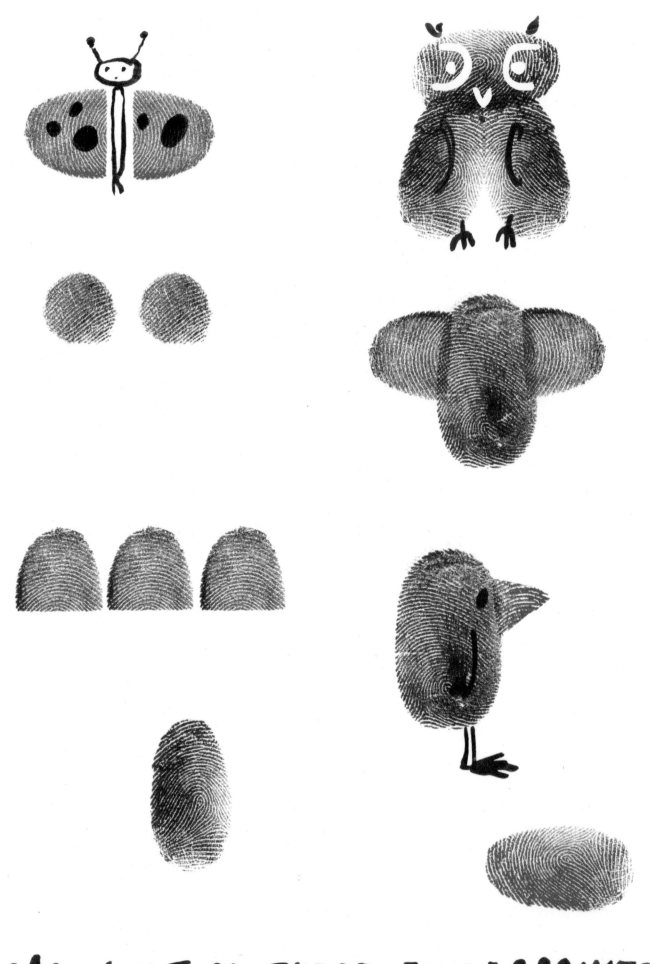

CAN YOU TURN THESE FINGERPRINTS

INTO CREATURES ?

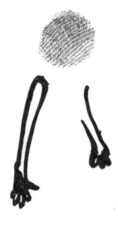

CAN YOU MAKE FINGERPRINT CHARACTERS?

CAN YOU MAKE MORE CHARACTERS?

COLOUR ME IN

RIP UP SOME COLOURED PAPER TO MAKE A FACE.

VAN GOGH

AFTER
VAN
GOGH

VINCENT VAN GOGH WAS BORN IN 1853 IN
THE NETHERLANDS.
ALTHOUGH HE PRODUCED MORE THAN 800 PAINTINGS
IN HIS SHORT LIFE, HE SOLD ONLY ONE. NOW HE IS
ONE OF THE MOST FAMOUS ARTISTS OF ALL TIME.

VAN GOGH PAINTED SUNFLOWERS TO EXPERIMENT
WITH COLOUR AND TO WELCOME GAUGUIN (A FELLOW
ARTIST) TO HIS STUDIO IN ARLES.
THE FRIENDSHIP DID NOT LAST AND VAN GOGH, WHO
WAS MENTALLY ILL, CUT OFF HIS EAR, AND A YEAR
LATER SHOT HIMSELF.

COLOUR IN THIS VASE OF SUNFLOWERS
USING AS MANY DIFFERENT KINDS OF
YELLOWS AND ORANGES AS YOU
CAN MAKE.
EXPERIMENT BY ADDING TINY AMOUNTS OF
OTHER COLOURS TO YOUR YELLOW AND ORANGE.

YELLOW OCHRE

YELLOW OCHRE IS THE OLDEST YELLOW. THE OCHRE CLAY IS MINED FROM THE GROUND, WASHED TO SEPARATE THE SAND FROM THE OCHRE, THEN DRIED IN THE SUN.

Modern chemistry led to the creation of new yellows.

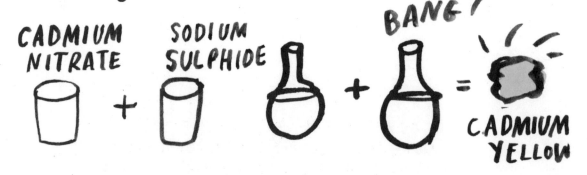

CADMIUM NITRATE + SODIUM SULPHIDE + BANG! = CADMIUM YELLOW

YELLOW IS ASSOCIATED WITH
ILLNESS, COWARDICE and CAUTION.

yellow →

TRAFFIC
LIGHTS

COLOUR IN THE
'YELLOW TANG' FISH.
IT IS A SALT WATER FISH FROM THE
SOUTH PACIFIC OCEANS NEAR HAWAII.
IT HAS 2 WHITE SPIKES ON THE SIDES
OF ITS TAIL. IT WILL USE THEM TO 'STAB'
ANOTHER FISH IF ATTACKED.

COLOUR EXPERIMENT NO.1
COLOUR WHEEL

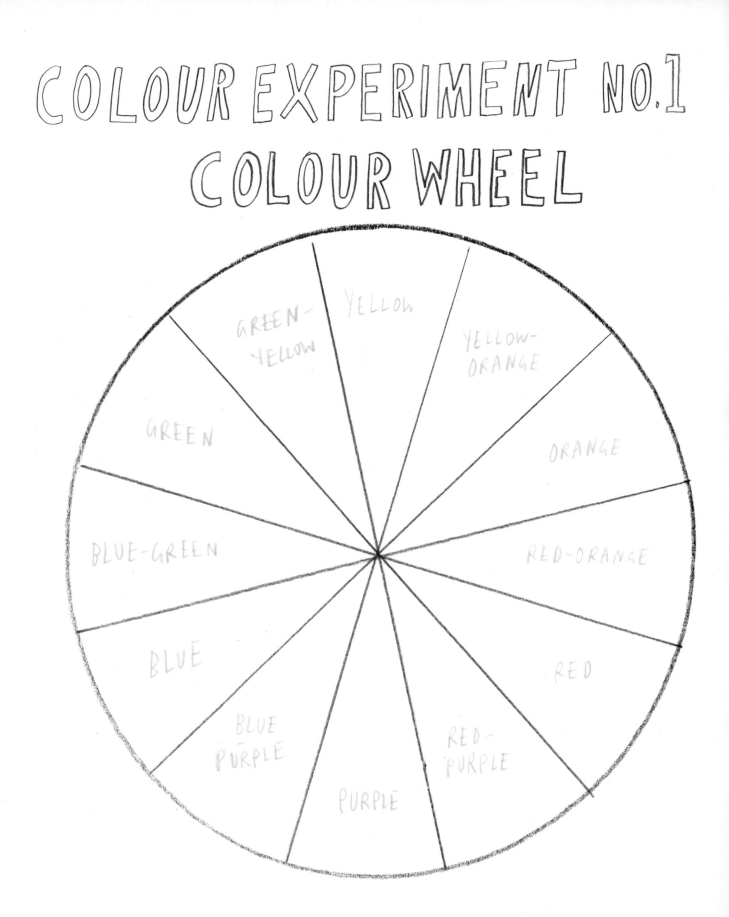

COLOUR THIS COLOUR WHEEL
USING WATERCOLOURS.

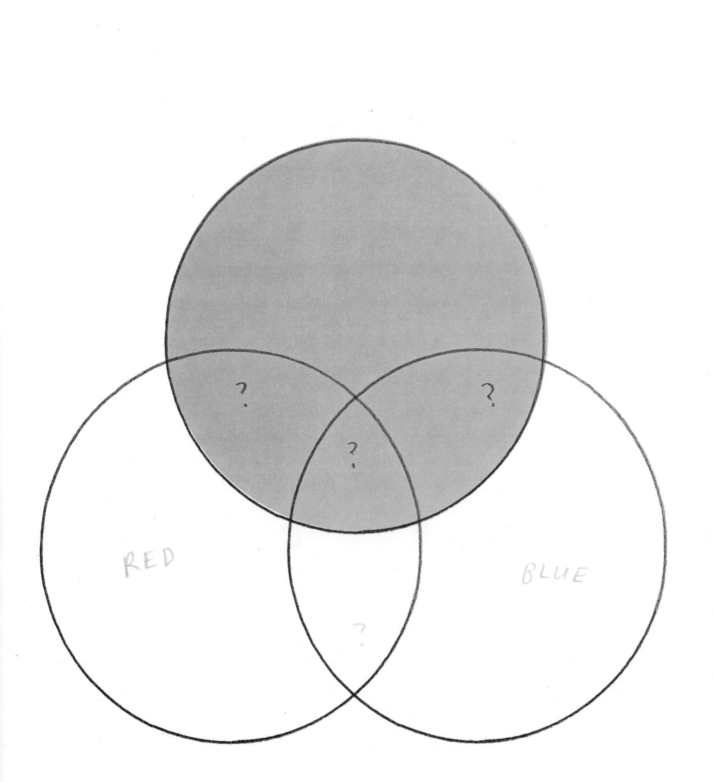

WHAT NEW COLOURS DO
YOU SEE WHEN YOU
MIX THESE COLOURS?

LIGHT
SOURCE

The darkest
part of the
shadow is
not on the
edge, but a
little way in.

DRAW WHERE
YOU THINK THE
SHADOW SHOULD
BE IF THE LIGHT
IS HERE.

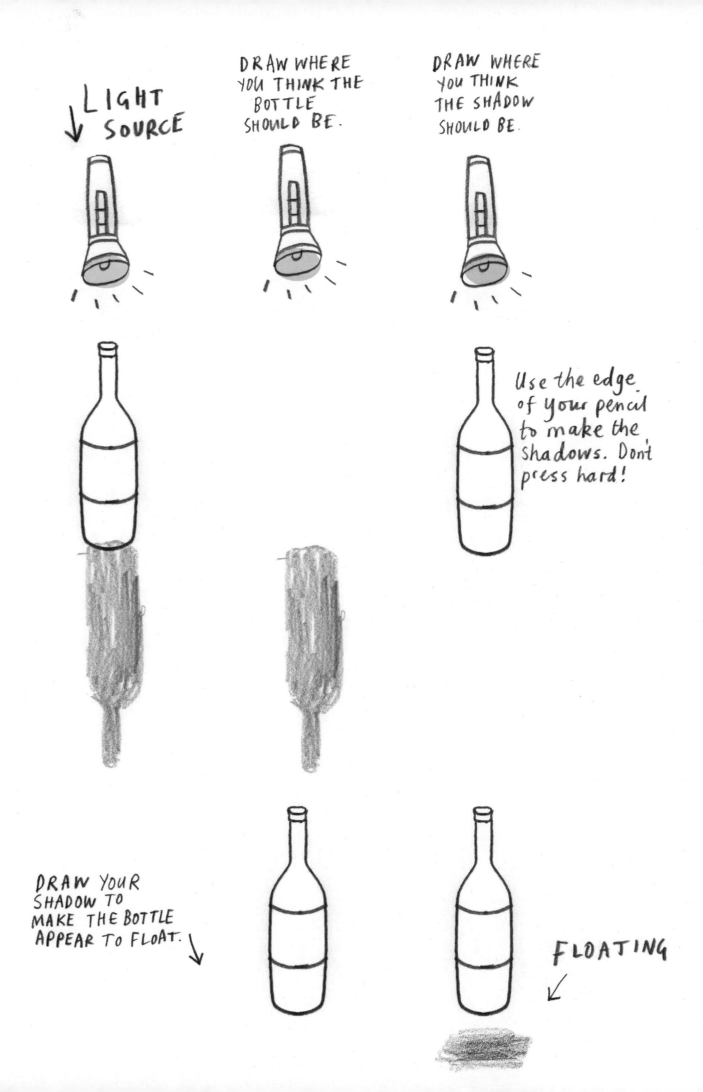

LIGHT SOURCE

DRAW WHERE YOU THINK THE BOTTLE SHOULD BE.

DRAW WHERE YOU THINK THE SHADOW SHOULD BE.

Use the edge of your pencil to make the shadows. Don't press hard!

DRAW YOUR SHADOW TO MAKE THE BOTTLE APPEAR TO FLOAT.

FLOATING

MAKE YOUR OWN
POSTCARD

IMAGINE YOU ARE ON HOLIDAY IN YOUR **OWN** TOWN, CITY OR VILLAGE.

LOOK AT EVERYTHING AROUND YOU AS IF FOR THE FIRST TIME.

DRAW SOMETHING YOU SEE OR LIKE ON THE FRONT OF THE POSTCARD AND ON THE BACK, WRITE ABOUT IT TO A FRIEND.

Post Card

CUT OUT
AND GLUE TOGETHER

THIS STRANGE POT PLANT HAS GROWN HUGE. IT IS GROWING OUT OF THE ROOM! DRAW IT.

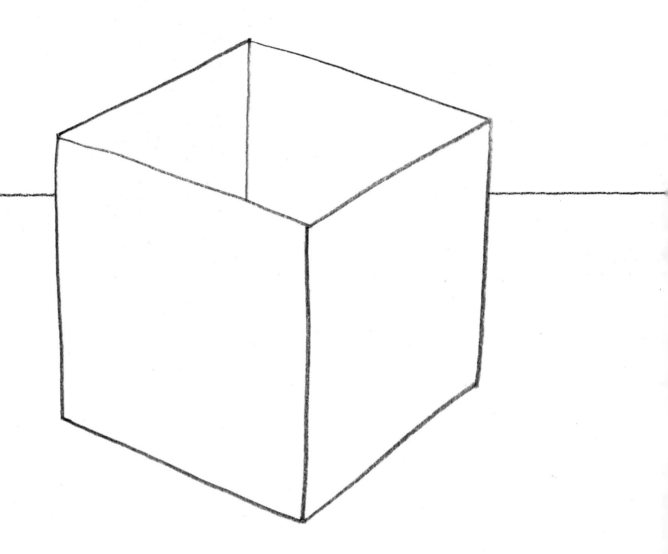

DRAW SOMETHING
CLIMBING OUT
OF THE BOX.

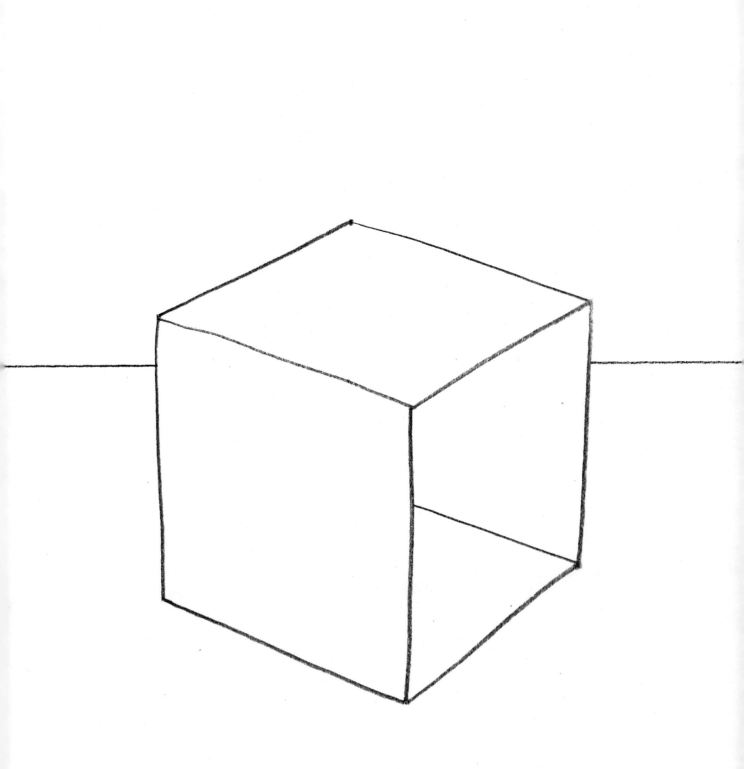

DRAW SOMETHING GOING INTO THE BOX.

DRAWING WITH AN ERASER

WHAT YOU WILL NEED.

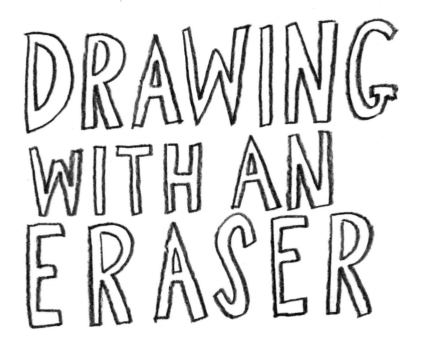

REGULAR HARD ERASER

OR A

SOFT 'PUTTY' ERASER

← CAN BE SQUEEZED INTO DIFFERENT SHAPES.

SOFT PENCIL OR

CHARCOAL OR

A GRAPHITE STICK

COVER THE PAGE WITH THE EDGE OF YOUR PENCIL OR GRAPHITE STICK. THEN USE AN ERASER TO DRAW!

START HERE
↙

MATISSE

HENRI MATISSE WAS BORN IN FRANCE IN 1869.
MATISSE IS KNOWN FOR WORK USING EXTRA-
ORDINARY BOLD COLOURS.
AFTER AN ART SHOW IN 1905, CRITICS
STARTED CALLING HIM A 'Fauve'. THIS MEANS
'wild beast' IN FRENCH!

WHEN HE WAS OLDER, MATISSE'S HEALTH
BEGAN TO FAIL. CONFINED TO A WHEELCHAIR,
HE STARTED MAKING 'Collages' IN A TECHNIQUE
HE CALLED "Painting with scissors".

MAKE YOUR OWN MATISSE-INSPIRED COLLAGE.

WHAT YOU WILL NEED.

A PENCIL
1 SHEET WHITE PAPER
1 SMALLER SQUARE OF COLOURED PAPER
     (OR COLOUR YOUR OWN, BOTH SIDES)
     (WITH PAINT BRUSH OR ROLLER.)

GLUE
SCISSORS

DRAW SOME SHAPES IN PENCIL AND
THEN CUT THEM OUT FROM THE
EDGES OF THE COLOURED SQUARE PAPER

ONCE YOU HAVE CUT OUT ALL YOUR SHAPES
STICK THE REMAINING SQUARE PAPER
WITH GLUE ONTO THE LARGER WHITE
PAPER.

FLIP OVER

NOW FLIP OVER THE SHAPES YOU HAVE CUT
OUT AND GLUE THEM NEXT TO THE SPACES
THEY WERE CUT FROM TO MAKE POSITIVE/NEGATIVE SHAPES

SEE HOW THE WHITE (NEGATIVE) SPACE
IS JUST AS IMPORTANT AS THE (POSITIVE) COLOURED SHAPES.

MATISSE-INSPIRED COLLAGE.

EXPERIMENT FURTHER BY USING TWO COLOURED
SQUARES, OR CHANGE THE BACKGROUND WHITE
PAPER TO A CONTRASTING COLOUR.

WINDOWS?

TURN THESE SHAPES INTO CHARACTERS

COLOUR EXPERIMENT. NO. 2

WHAT YOU NEED

MIRROR
WATER CONTAINER
OR GLASS BOWL

WHITE PAPER
BLACK PAPER
SCISSORS
STICKY TAPE

CUT OUT CIRCLE
OF BLACK PAPER. THEN
CUT OUT A LITTLE
HOLE IN THE MIDDLE
AND TAPE OVER TOP
OF TORCH.

SHINE THE TORCH ON THE MIRROR
AND SEE THE RAINBOW APPEAR
ON THE WHITE PAPER.

MIRROR
AT AN
ANGLE

3/4 WATER FILL

CONTAINER
WITH WATER

White
Paper to
Catch
rainbow

COLOUR RED IN BLUE

COLOUR YELLOW IN GREEN

COLOUR BLUE IN RED

COLOUR GREEN IN YELLOW

NOW READ THE _COLOURS_ YOU SEE, _NOT_ THE WORDS.

LAPIS (BLUE) LAZULI

THE RENAISSANCE MASTERS CRUSHED
LAPIS LAZULI ROCKS INTO POWDER
AND MIXED IT WITH OIL TO MAKE AN
INTENSE BLUE.
MANY PAINTINGS OF THE 'MADONNA'
USE THIS PIGMENT.

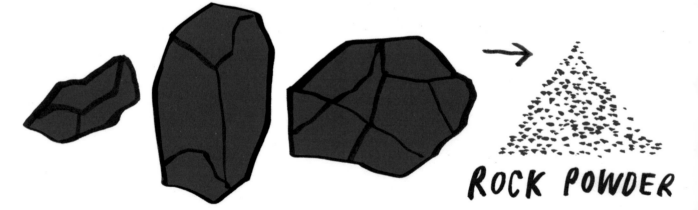

ROCK POWDER

DURING THE Renaissance
LAPIZ LAZULI WAS MORE
EXPENSIVE THAN GOLD.

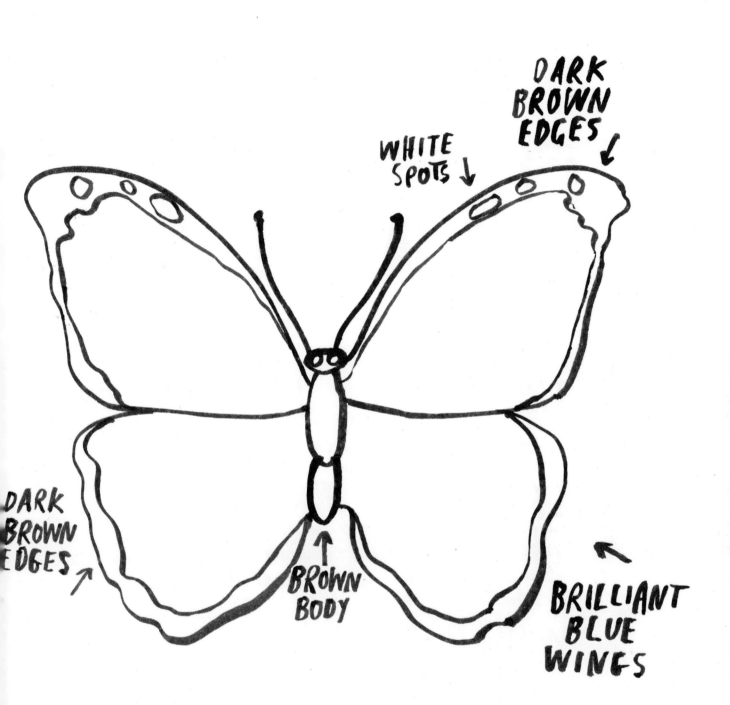

WHITE SPOTS ↓

DARK BROWN EDGES ↓

DARK BROWN EDGES ↑

BROWN BODY ↑

BRILLIANT BLUE WINGS ↖

COLOUR IN THIS BLUE MORPHO BUTTERFLY

TYRIAN PURPLE

THOUSANDS of PURPURA SNAILS  WERE CRUSHED TO PRODUCE THIS HIGHLY PRIZED PIGMENT of THE ANCIENT WORLD

CLEOPATRA ORDERED THOUSANDS OF SNAILS TO BE CRUSHED to make a A FEW PRECIOUS OUNCES

COLOUR CLEOPATRA WITH PURPLE

ALEXANDER CALDER

WAS BORN IN THE USA in 1898. HE WAS AN ARTISTIC
PIONEER WHO CREATED THE ART FORM CALLED
THE 'MOBILE'.   SOME OF CALDER'S MOBILES
OR SCULPTURES ARE TINY, WHILE OTHERS
ARE HUGE.

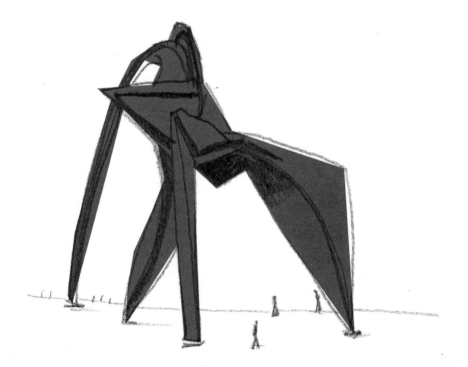

HIS 50-TON RED ABSTRACT SCULPTURE
IN CHICAGO'S FEDERAL SQUARE, CALLED
'Flamingo' IS ONE OF HIS MOST FAMOUS WORKS.

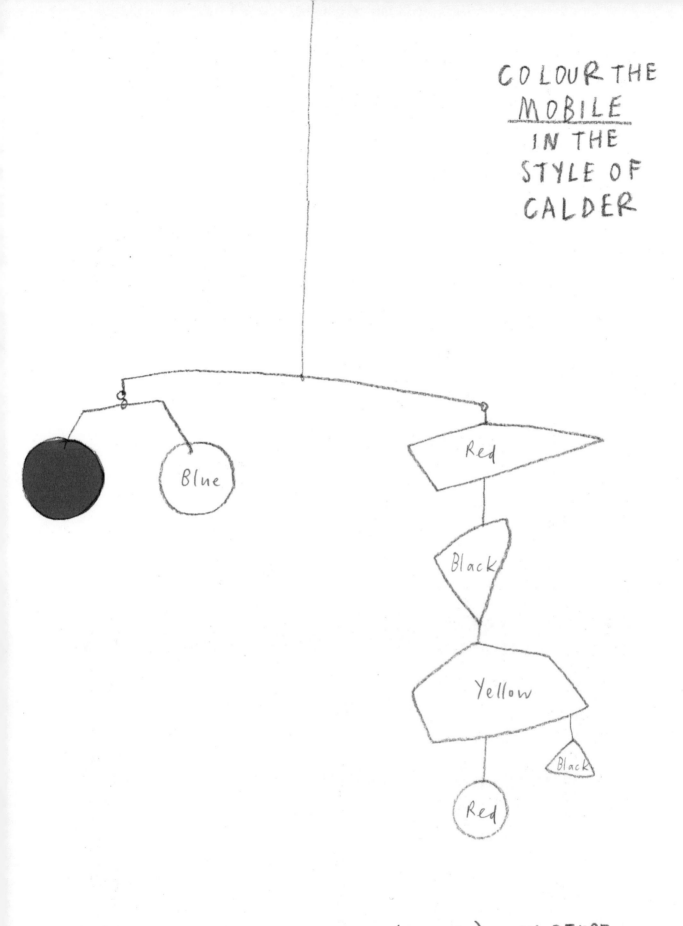

COLOUR THE
MOBILE
IN THE
STYLE OF
CALDER

Blue

Red

Black

Yellow

Black

Red

HE MADE MOBILES, KINETIC (MOVING) SCULPTURE
OR
STABILES, NON-MOVING SCULPTURE

THE 'FLAMINGO' IS A 'STABILES' SCULPTURE.

MAKE A 'MOBILE'

WHAT YOU WILL NEED:

PAPER CLIPS
THREAD OR STRING
CARD / CARD SHAPES
3 STRAWS (PAPER ONES WORK BEST)
OR TIGHTLY ROLL
SOME PAPER.
SCISSORS

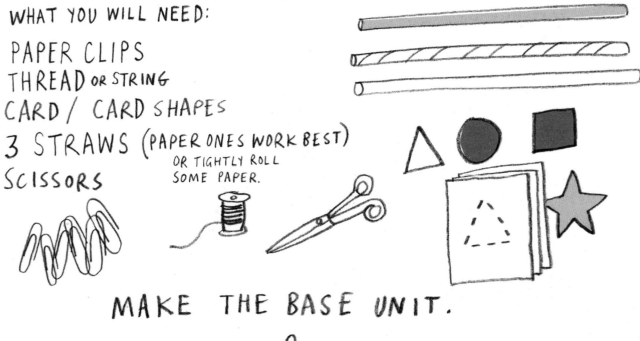

MAKE THE BASE UNIT.

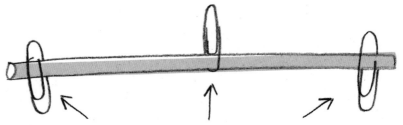

SLIP A PAPER CLIP ONTO THE MIDDLE OF THE STRAW.
PUT 2 MORE NEAR THE END OF THE STRAW.
MAKE 2 MORE UNITS.
PUT THEM TOGETHER USING PAPER CLIP CHAINS.

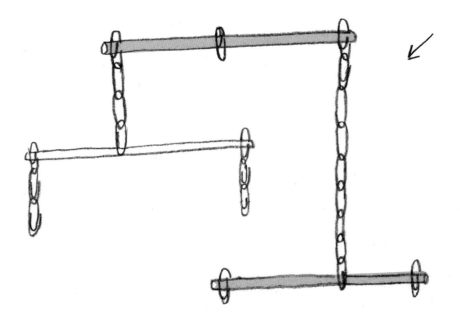

CUT OUT THIN CARD SHAPES. CALDER LIKED
TO USE SIMPLE GEOMETRIC SHAPES; SQUARE
CIRCLE, RECTANGLE.

CLIP THE SHAPES TO THE MOBILE AND HANG
FROM CEILING.

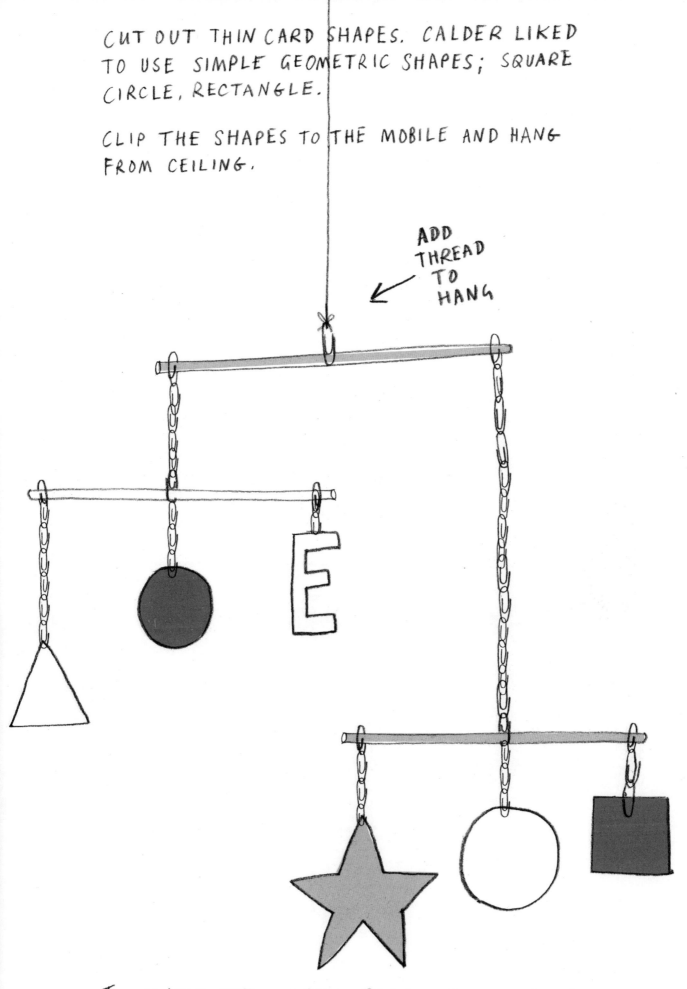

ADD
THREAD
TO
HANG

TO MAKE THE MOBILE BALANCE, SLIDE and
ADJUST THE PAPER CLIPS.

EXIT

DRAW OR PAINT something 3D in

THIS ART GALLERY. DRAW LOTS OF LITTLE THINGS.

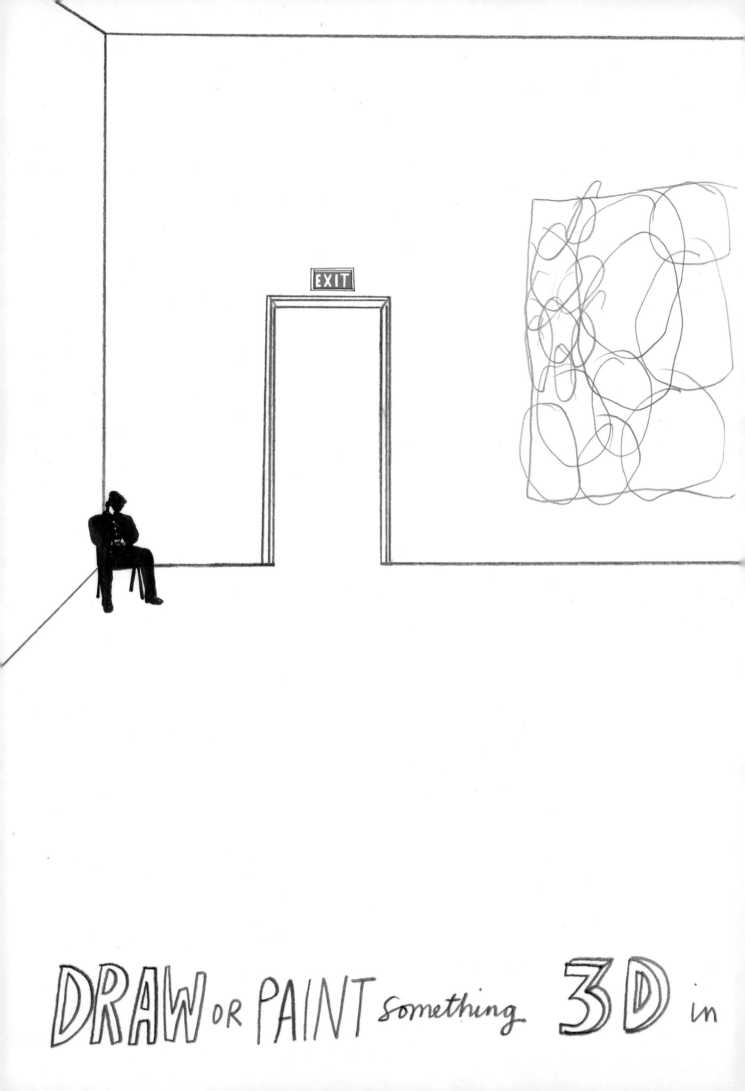

DRAW OR PAINT something 3D in

THIS ART GALLERY. DRAW ONE BIG THING.

COLOUR IN

DESIGN YOUR OWN HOUSE

THIS PLINTH IS
MADE OF GLASS.
DRAW SOMETHING
MADE OF WOOD
ON TOP OF IT.

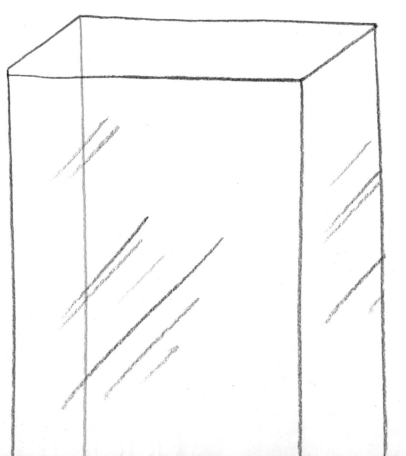

THIS PLINTH IS
MADE OF STONE.
DRAW SOMETHING
MADE OF GLASS
ON TOP OF IT.

DRAW
SOMETHING
OLD
ON THIS
PLINTH.

DRAW
SOMETHING
MODERN
ON THIS
PLINTH.

JACKSON POLLOCK

BORN IN 1912 IN THE USA.
JACKSON POLLOCK IS FAMOUS
FOR DRIPPING AND SPLASHING
PAINT ONTO CANVAS.

MAKE YOUR OWN

JACKSON POLLOCK.

Lay a sheet of
paper in the bottom
of a box. Dip a
marble into paint
and drop into box.

Roll the marble
around. Repeat
with different
colours.

COLOUR EXPERIMENT NO. 3

What you will need.

CARD

SCISSORS

PAINTS
PENS

SHORT
PENCIL

A COMPASS
OR A JAR
LID TO
MAKE THE
CIRCLE SHAPE

CUT OUT A CIRCLE
OF CARD AND
DECORATE WITH
PAINT, PENS OR
STICKERS.

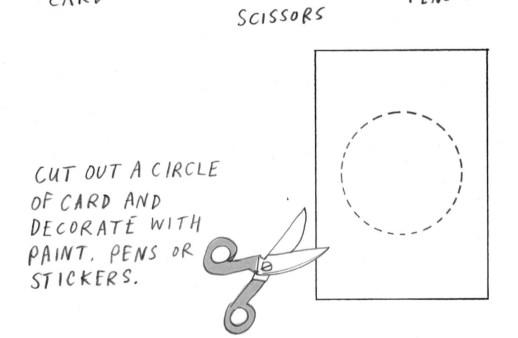

MAKE A HOLE IN THE CENTRE
AND PUSH A SHORT PENCIL THROUGH,
SPIN...
WHAT HAPPENS TO THE COLOURS?

[   ] ← Answer

and your OWN·T-SHIRT

FINGERPRINTS
& PAPER CUT-OUTS

ADD YOUR OWN FINGERPRINTS
TO THESE CUT-OUTS.
THEN MAKE YOUR OWN CUT-OUT
FIGURES.

MAKE UP YOUR OWN COMIC

DRAW A SKELETON
USING A WHITE
PENCIL OR CRAYON.

DRAW A SKELETON
USING A BLACK
PENCIL OR CRAYON.

COLOUR THIS GRID WITH A PATTERN
USING 3 COLOURS.

MONDRIAN

BORN IN THE NETHERLANDS IN 1872.
PIET MONDRIAN IS MOST FAMOUS FOR
HIS PAINTINGS OF RECTANGLES OF
WHITE AND PRIMARY COLOURS DISSECTED
BY STRONG BLACK LINES.
HE HELPED FORM THE DE STIJL
MOVEMENT WHICH BELIEVED THE
FOUNDATION OF ALL THINGS COULD BE
FOUND IN THE SIMPLEST OF FORMS,
LIKE PRIMARY COLOURS AND STRAIGHT
LINES.

MAKE YOUR OWN
MONDRIAN-INSPIRED
DRAWING.

COLOUR IN THE SHAPES
WITH RED, YELLOW
AND BLUE WHERE MARKED.

yell

blue

red

red

yellow

COLOUR THIS GRID WITH A PATTERN
USING 5 COLOURS.

TANGRAM

Tangrams ARE ANCIENT CHINESE PUZZLES.
THEY ARE MADE OF 7 MOVABLE GEOMETRIC
SHAPES.
THE IDEA OF THIS PUZZLE IS TO USE ALL 7
PIECES (OR TANS) TO CREATE A PICTURE OR
DESIGN.

USE THE TEMPLATE ON THE OPPOSITE PAGE TO
MAKE YOUR OWN TANGRAMS.
HERE ARE SOME IDEAS:

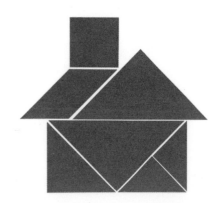

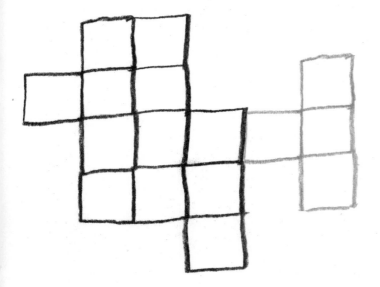

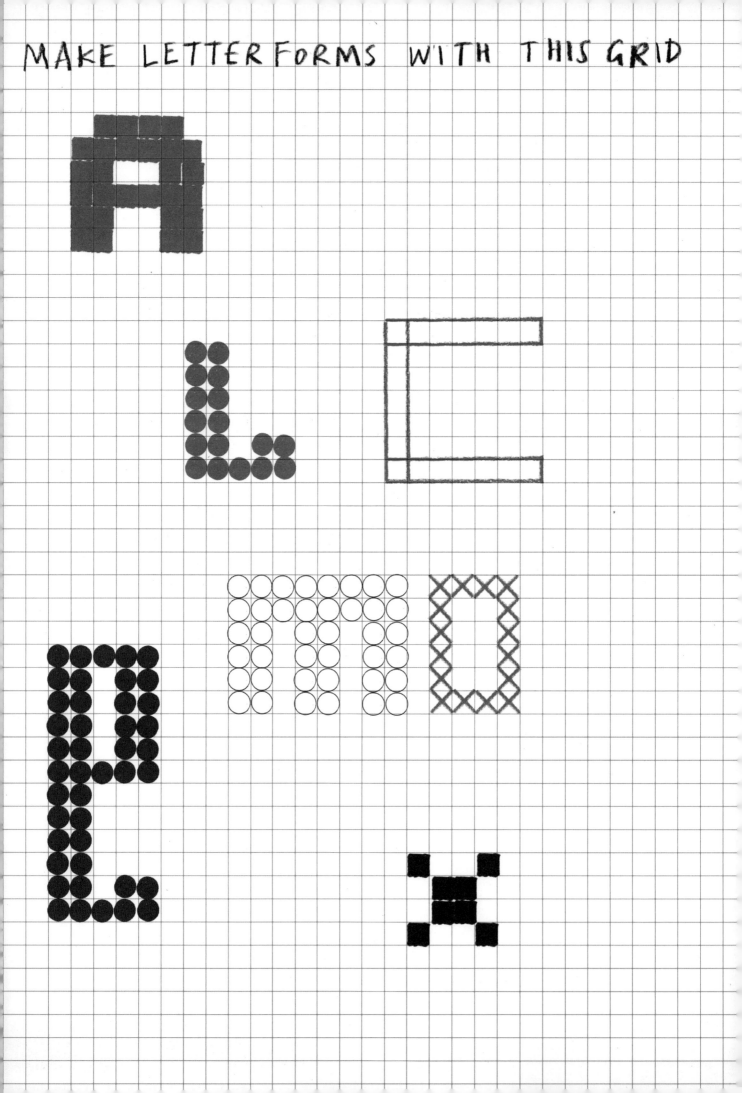

MAKE LETTERFORMS WITH THIS GRID

CONTINUE THESE TRIANGLES TO FILL THE PAGES.

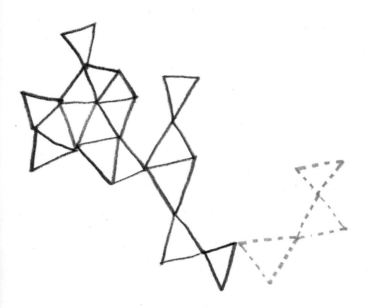

MÖBIUS STRIP

Also called the 'twisted cylinder'
The Möbius strip only has one surface.

1. Take a strip of paper.
2. Give it a half twist (turn one end over)
3. Tape the ends together.

You have now made a Möbius strip

Put it in front of you and
try to draw it. The more
you try, the easier it will
become.

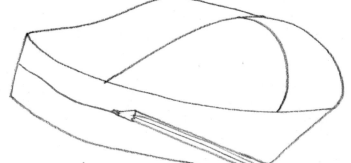

CURIOUS
EXPERIMENT.
Draw a pencil line around the paper ring.
You will find the line on both the outside
and inside of the ring, even though you
have not lifted your pencil.

CIRCLES

DRAW CIRCLES BY HAND

SEE HOW PERFECTLY CIRCULAR YOU CAN BE.

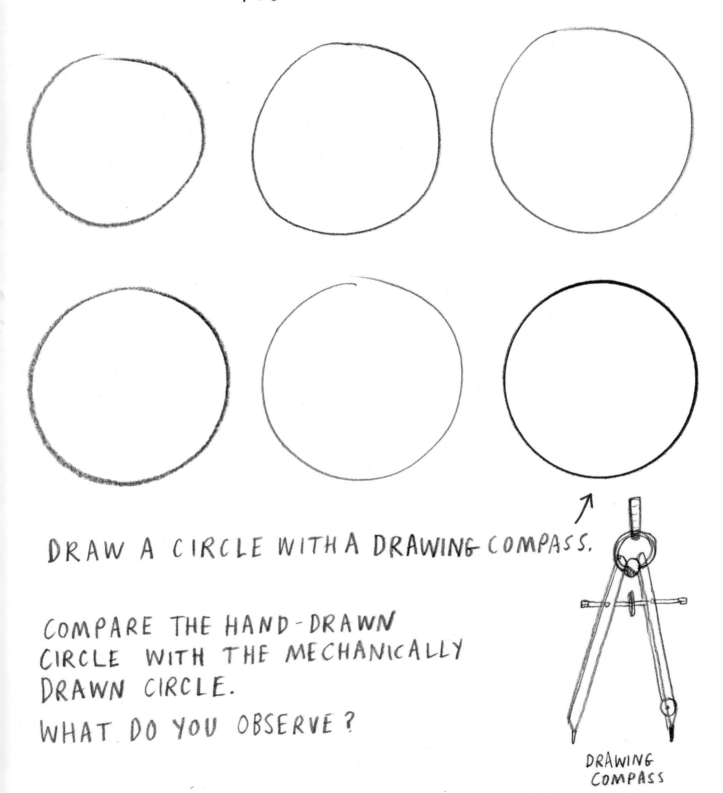

DRAW A CIRCLE WITH A DRAWING COMPASS.

COMPARE THE HAND-DRAWN
CIRCLE WITH THE MECHANICALLY
DRAWN CIRCLE.

WHAT DO YOU OBSERVE?

DRAWING
COMPASS

PAUL KLEE

BORN IN SWITZERLAND in 1879
HE WAS AN ARTIST, A MUSICIAN,
WRITER AND A POET. AND ONE OF
THE MOST ORIGINAL MASTERS OF
MODERN ART.

After Klee

PAUL KLEE SAID THAT
"DRAWING WAS LIKE TAKING A LINE FOR A WALK."

TAKE A LINE FOR A WALK
(PAUL KLEE)

WITH A PENCIL, TAKE YOUR PENCIL FOR A WALK.
DRAW WITHOUT TAKING IT OFF THE PAPER.

THIS TIME USE A WHITE PENCIL

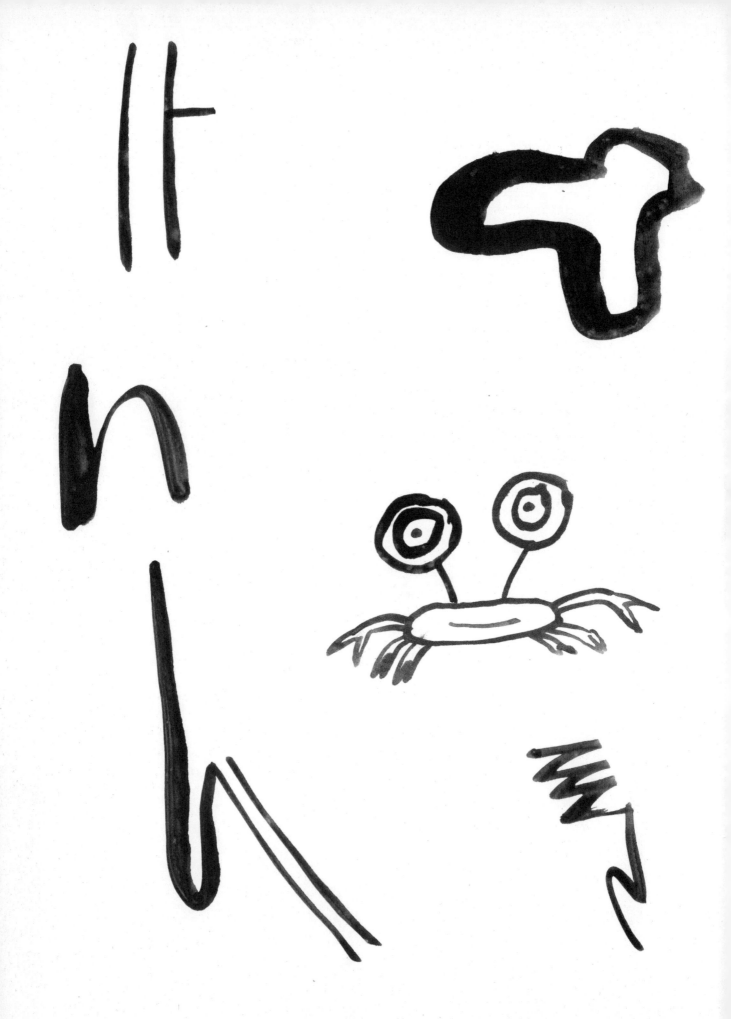

TURN THESE ABSTRACT DOODLES INTO

SOMETHING. 'Look, I've made a crab.'

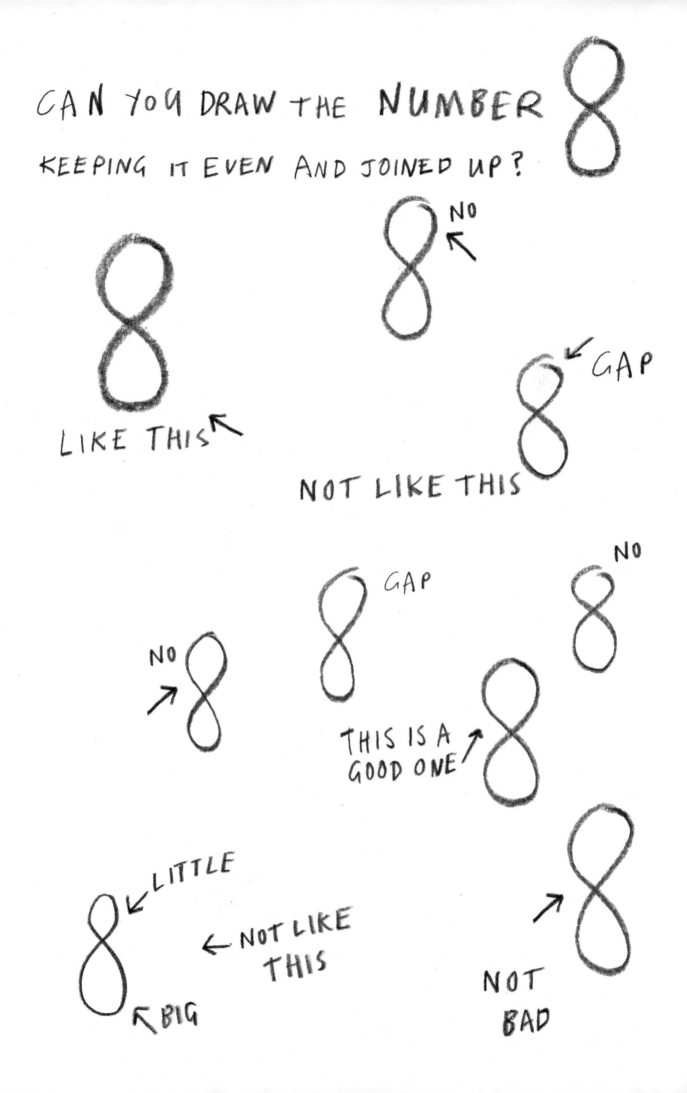

CAN YOU DRAW THE NUMBER 8

KEEPING IT EVEN AND JOINED UP?

NO

LIKE THIS

GAP

NOT LIKE THIS

NO

GAP

NO

THIS IS A GOOD ONE

LITTLE

← NOT LIKE THIS

← BIG

NOT BAD

FILL THE PAGE.

↓

FILL THE PAGE.

MARK MAKING WITH CARD

WHAT YOU NEED.

INK OR PAINT

PIECE OF CARD

SMALL FLAT TRAY
OR PLATE FOR INK

PAPER

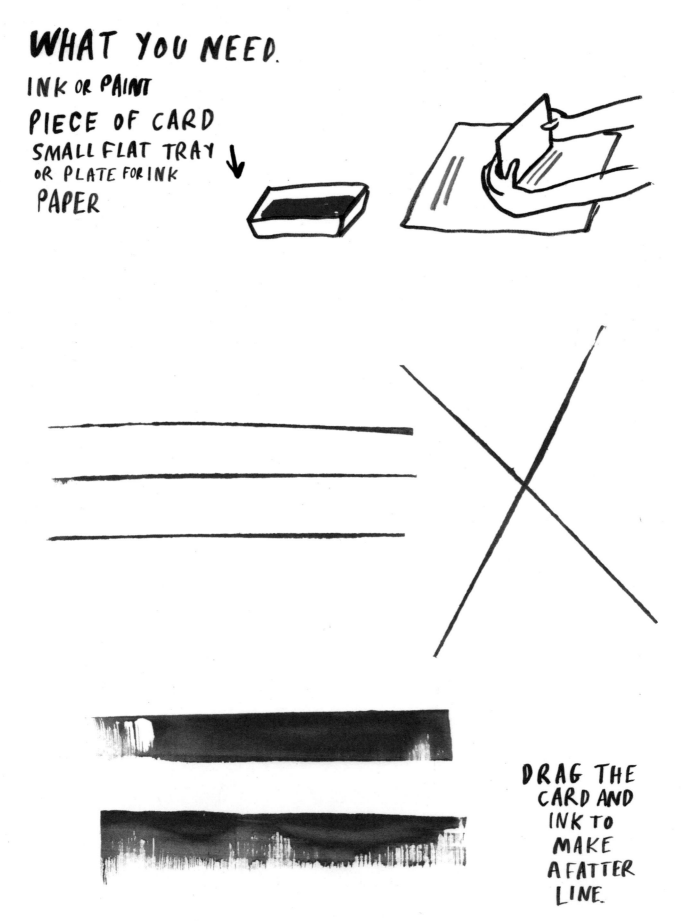

DRAG THE
CARD AND
INK TO
MAKE
A FATTER
LINE.

MAKE A GRID

BEND THE CARD

MAKE PATTERNS

WHEN OBJECTS OR PEOPLE ARE DRAWN
SMALL, THEY LOOK FAR AWAY.

WHEN THEY ARE BIGGER, THEY LOOK NEARER.

TRY TO DRAW SOME PEOPLE
SMALL - (FAR AWAY)
MEDIUM - (MIDDLE DISTANCE)
BIG - (VERY NEAR)

FAR AWAY

MEDIUM

BIG

HORIZON
LINE

WHAT are they HOLDING UP?

WHAT SUPERHERO IS LIFTING
THE CAR?

LEARN HOW TO DO HATCHING

FIVE LITTLE LINES, Change direction, FIVE LITTLE LINES.
Change direction, FIVE LITTLE LINES......

LEAVE A
'PEEP' HOLE
AND DRAW SOMETHING IN IT.

HATCHING AND CROSSHATCHING

HATCHING IS A DRAWING TECHNIQUE USING PARALLEL LINES DRAWN CLOSELY TOGETHER TO CREATE TONE, SHADE OR TEXTURE WITH LINES ONLY.

CROSSHATCHING IS A DRAWING TECHNIQUE MADE OF PARALLEL LINES ON TOP OF EACH OTHER.

TO CROSSHATCH WITH PEN OR PENCIL, DRAW LINES SIDE BY SIDE, THEN ON TOP OF EACH OTHER TO MAKE TONE OR SHADING EFFECTS.

HATCHING

STEP.1   STEP.2   STEP.3

CROSSHATCHING

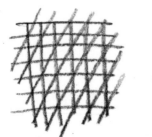

← ON TOP OF EACH OTHER TO CREATE 'TONE'

STEPS 1,2,3

REPEATING STEPS 1, 2 AND 3.

TRY YOUR OWN CROSSHATCHING EXPERIMENTS
IN THESE BOXES.

IN THIS BOX, CROSSHATCH UNTIL THE BOX BECOMES
VERY DARK. TO DO THIS, KEEP REPEATING
STEPS 1, 2 AND 3.

CONTINUE THESE CIRCLES TO FILL THE PAGES.

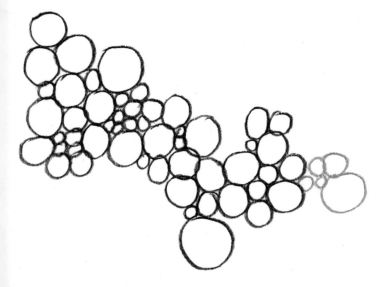

EMPTY
YOUR POCKETS

BAG OF NUTS AND SCREWS

SPINNING TOP

KEY,

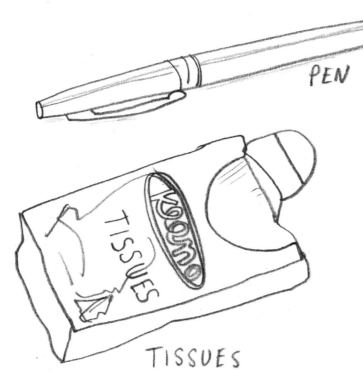

PEN

TISSUES

USED TISSUE

HERE'S WHAT'S IN MINE

DRAW WHAT IS
IN THEM. AND COLOUR
THEM IN

↓

LOUISE BOURGEOIS

LOUISE BOURGEOIS WAS BORN IN FRANCE IN 1911.
SHE MOVED TO AMERICA IN THE LATE 30s AND
TURNED TO SCULPTURE.

SHE IS MOST WELL KNOWN FOR HER SPIDER
SCULPTURES CALLED 'Maman' (MOTHER)

'Maman'

" WHY THE SPIDER? BECAUSE MY BEST
FRIEND WAS MY MOTHER AND SHE WAS
DELIBERATE, NEAT, CLEVER, PATIENT,
INDISPENSABLE AND AS USEFUL AS A SPIDER".
Louise Bourgeois.

MAKE YOUR OWN 'SPIDERS'
BY DROPPING BLOBS OF INK THEN
BLOWING ON THEM THROUGH A STRAW.

HAND & FINGER PRINTS
WHAT YOU NEED TO MAKE THEM:
PAINT, COLOURED PENCILS.
PAPER, HANDS, IMAGINATION!

LET'S MAKE MORE OF THEM!

↓

DRAW SOME SLEEPING CREATURES.

DRAW SOME SLEEPING CREATURES AT NIGHT.

RAW WHAT YOU SEE THROUGH THE KEYHOLE.

MAGRITTE

RENÉ MAGRITTE WAS A SURREALIST PAINTER WHO WAS BORN IN BELGIUM IN 1898.
MAGRITTE'S PAINTINGS ARE MYSTERIOUS AND MAGICAL. HE PUTS ORDINARY THINGS TOGETHER THAT DON'T BELONG TOGETHER TO CHANGE THEIR MEANING.

AFTER MAGRITTE

'LE FAUX MIROIR' (THE FALSE MIRROR)

MAGRITTE REPLACES THE IRIS WITH A CLOUD-FILLED SKY.

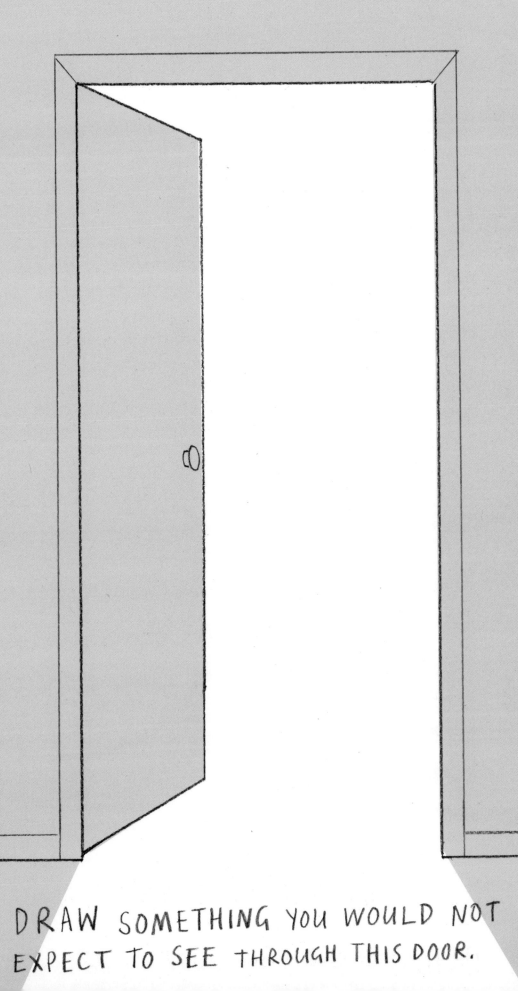

DRAW SOMETHING YOU WOULD NOT
EXPECT TO SEE THROUGH THIS DOOR.

DRAW WHAT THIS MAN IS DREAMING OF.

DRAW SOMEONE OR SOMETHING DREAMING
OF THIS MAN.

WHAT IS HE LOOKING
AT TO MAKE HIM SO
SURPRISED?

WHAT IS HE TOO SCARED TO LOOK AT?

TURN these PEOPLE into.... ALIENS

and DRAW their SPACESHIP.

Draw a SHARK in the TANK.

DRAW YOUR
OWN FACE
AS MODERN
ART.

CREATE YOUR OWN
GALLERY OF PICTURES.

DRAW A MAP FROM YOUR HOUSE TO SCHOOL
SHOWING 3 THINGS YOU ALWAYS SEE.
IN 5 MINUTES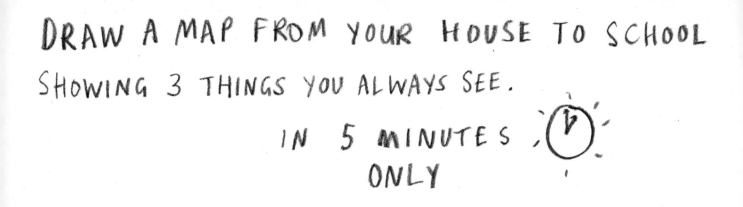
ONLY

FILL THIS PAGE WITH ALL DIFFERENT DRAWINGS
OF CLOCKS. USE YOUR IMAGINATION!

FLAT CLOCKS
SCARY CLOCKS
RUNNING CLOCKS
SMALL CLOCKS
BIG CLOCKS
HAIRY CLOCKS

FROTTAGE

COMES FROM A FRENCH WORD 'Frotter,' TO RUB.
IN FROTTAGE THE ARTIST USES A PENCIL
OR GRAPHITE STICK AND MAKES A <u>RUBBING</u>
OVER A TEXTURED SURFACE.

HERE I'VE USED SOME COINS,
PAPER CLIPS AND STRING.

PAPER CLIPS

PENCIL
SHARPENER

METAL SHELVING.

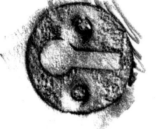

KEYHOLE

COINS.

STRING.

USE THE EDGE
of your pencil and
MAKE SOME RUBBINGS
OF <u>EVERYTHING</u> AROUND YOU.

WOOD

THIS IS A
MAGIC
MOUNTAIN.
DRAW WHAT YOU
THINK IS
INSIDE.

DRAW HOW YOU WOULD FEEL
IF YOU WENT INSIDE IT.

↓

BRIDGET RILEY

BORN IN 1931 IN THE UNITED KINGDOM, BRIDGET RILEY WAS ONE OF THE LEADING PRACTITIONERS OF OP (OPTICAL) ART.

RILEY USED STRONG GEOMETRIC SHAPES IN BOTH BLACK AND WHITE AND COLOUR TO PRODUCE AMAZING SENSATIONS OF MOVEMENT AND ILLUSION.

SOME OF HER WORK IS SAID TO MAKE PEOPLE FEEL LIKE THEY ARE SKYDIVING, AND FOR OTHERS: SEA SICKNESS!

MAKE YOUR OWN OP ART DRAWING.

CUT A WAVE SHAPE OUT OF A PIECE OF CARDBOARD TO MAKE A 'TEMPLATE'. PUT THE TEMPLATE ON TOP OF A PIECE OF PAPER. MAKE SURE THE TEMPLATE IS A BIT BIGGER THAN THE PAPER YOU DRAW ON. USE THE TEMPLATE TO HELP YOU TO TRACE AROUND THE SHAPE, STARTING FROM THE RIGHT UNTIL YOU FINISH ON THE LEFT HAND SIDE.

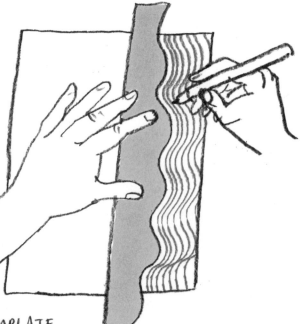

EXPERIMENT WITH DIFFERENT TEMPLATE SHAPES AND HOW CLOSE YOU DRAW THE LINES TOGETHER.

LINES

PRACTICE DRAWING STRAIGHT
LINES IN EQUAL LENGTH AND
WEIGHT, EQUALLY DIVIDED.

NOW TRY TO VARY THE WEIGHT.

EXPERIMENT WITH WEIGHT, SHAPE, SPACE.

CONTINUE THESE TRIANGLES TO FILL THE PAGE.

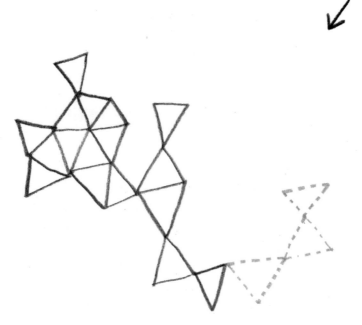

CONTINUE THESE LINES TO FILL THE PAGES.

COLOUR THIS GRID WITH A PATTERN

CONTINUE THESE RECTANGLES TO FILL THE PAGES.

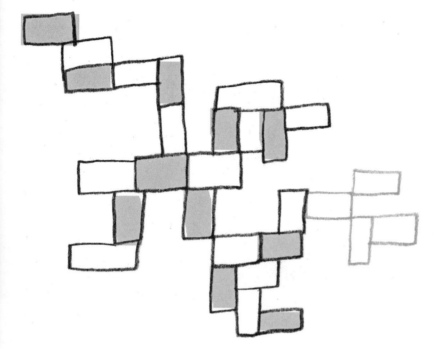

AFTER-IMAGE

LOOK AT THE CENTRE OF THE LIGHTBULB FOR 30 SECONDS, THEN LOOK AT THE FACING PAGE TO SEE A GLOWING LIGHTBULB! THIS IS CALLED an 'AFTER-IMAGE.'

NOW DO THE SAME THING AGAIN, BUT LOOK AT A BLANK WALL AFTERWARDS TO SEE A 'HUGE' GLOWING BULB.

CONTINUE THESE LINES TO FILL THE PAGES.

CONTINUE THESE LINES TO FILL THE PAGES.

PAINT OR COLOUR THIS CHAMELEON
SO THAT IT IS LOST IN THE BACKGROUND
MAKING IT CAMOUFLAGED.

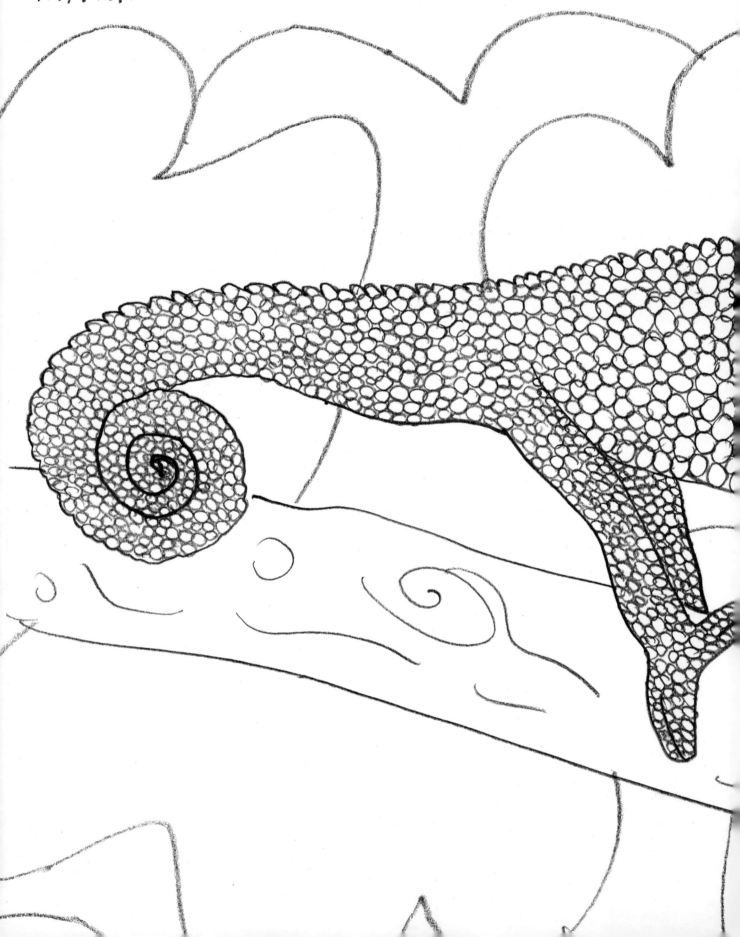

A — VERY LIGHT BROWN
B — LIGHT GREEN
C — BROWN
D — MEDIUM GREEN
E — VERY DARK GREEN

ANDY WARHOL

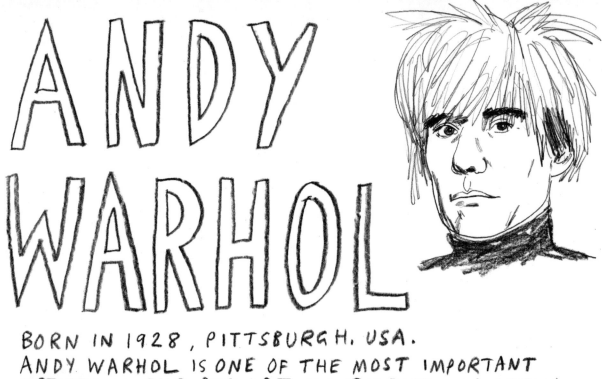

BORN IN 1928, PITTSBURGH. USA.
ANDY WARHOL IS ONE OF THE MOST IMPORTANT
ARTISTS IN THE POP ART MOVEMENT IN AMERICA.
HE ACHIEVED FAME LIKE NO OTHER ARTIST.
ONE OF HIS MOST FAMOUS QUOTES IS
   " In the future, everyone will be world-
   famous for 15 minutes"

THE SOUP CANS ARE PROBABLY THE MOST
RECOGNIZABLE IMAGES IN AMERICAN ART.

ANDY WARHOL TOLD PEOPLE HE PAINTED SOUP CANS
BECAUSE HE ATE SOUP FOR LUNCH EVERY DAY.

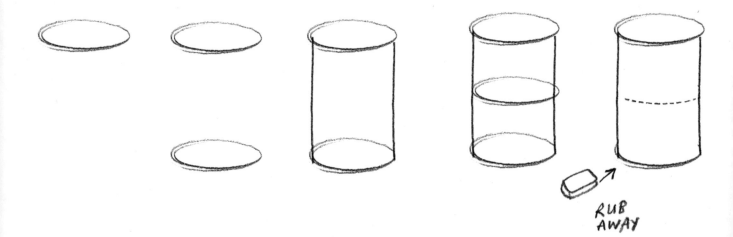

RUB
AWAY

FINISH THIS WARHOL-INSPIRED PAINTING USING
PAINTS OR COLOURED PENCILS.
CHANGE THE COLOUR OF EACH SOUP CAN AND EACH
SQUARE BACKGROUND. MAKE UP YOUR OWN SOUPS.

↗

TAKE OFF YOUR SHOE , PUT IT IN
FRONT OF YOU AND DRAW IT.

CARMINE RED

THE COLOUR CARMINE RED IS PRODUCED FROM 'Cochineal'. COCHINEAL IS A TINY INSECT FROM SOUTH AMERICA. 70,000 INSECTS NEED TO BE CRUSHED and DRIED TO PRODUCE 1 lb of COCHINEAL DYE.

× 70,000 = 1 lb CARMINE RED

TODAY THE MOST COMMON RED IS CALLED CADMIUM RED.

IT IS MADE FROM CHEMICALS.

COLOUR IN THIS BIRD
called a ROBIN (red breast.)

DRAW WHAT THESE PEOPLE ARE DREAMING ABOUT.

DO BIRDS DREAM TOO?
WHAT DO YOU THINK THEY DREAM ABOUT?

WHAT'S IN YOUR KITCHEN DRAWER?
CLOSE YOUR EYES....
TAKE OUT THE FIRST THREE THINGS YOU FIND
AND DRAW THEM.

HERE'S WHAT'S IN MINE.

PAPER GRIP
SAFETY PINS
CORRECTION FLUID

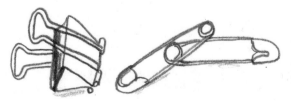

MAKE UP A STORY ABOUT THE
THREE OBJECTS.

IT STARTS WITH...

Rex put on one glove and opened
the drawer slowly....

DRAW WHAT HAS
MADE HER HAPPY.

WHO LIVES <u>ON TOP</u> OF THE MOUNTAIN?

WHO LIVES UNDER THE MOUNTAIN?

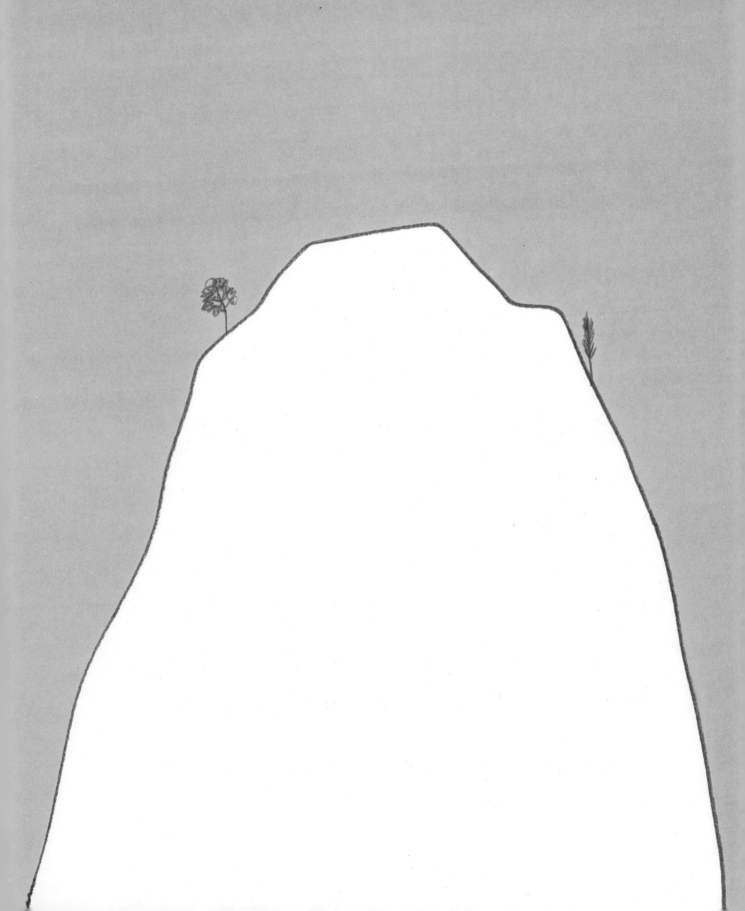

TRACE AROUND YOUR HAND.
NOW COLOUR IN USING PAINT
OR COLOURED PENCILS TO MATCH
THE COLOUR OF YOUR SKIN.

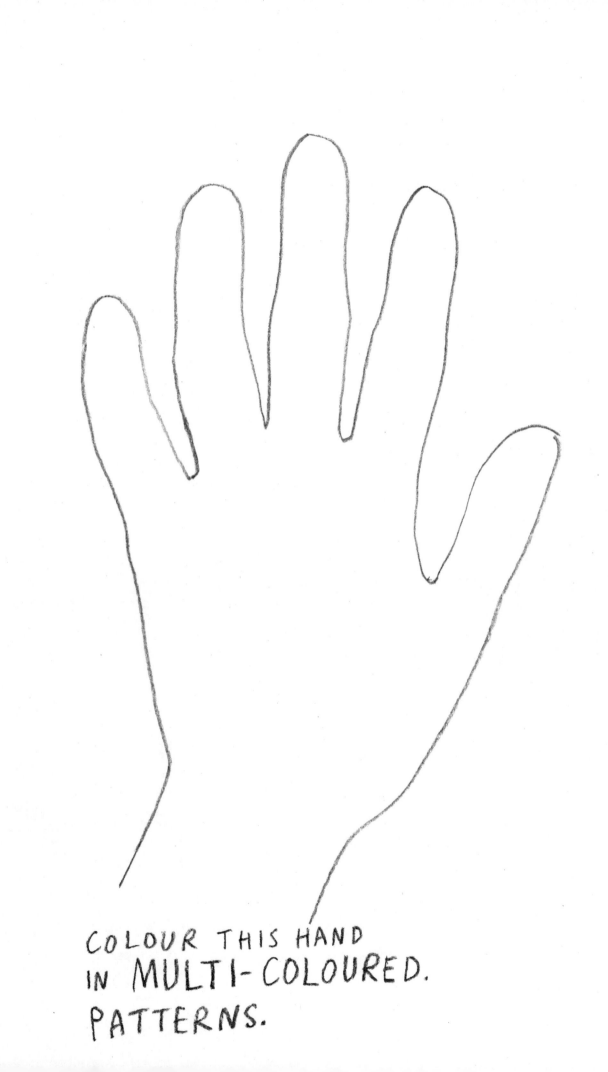

COLOUR THIS HAND
IN MULTI-COLOURED.
PATTERNS.

HOW TO DRAW A BICYCLE

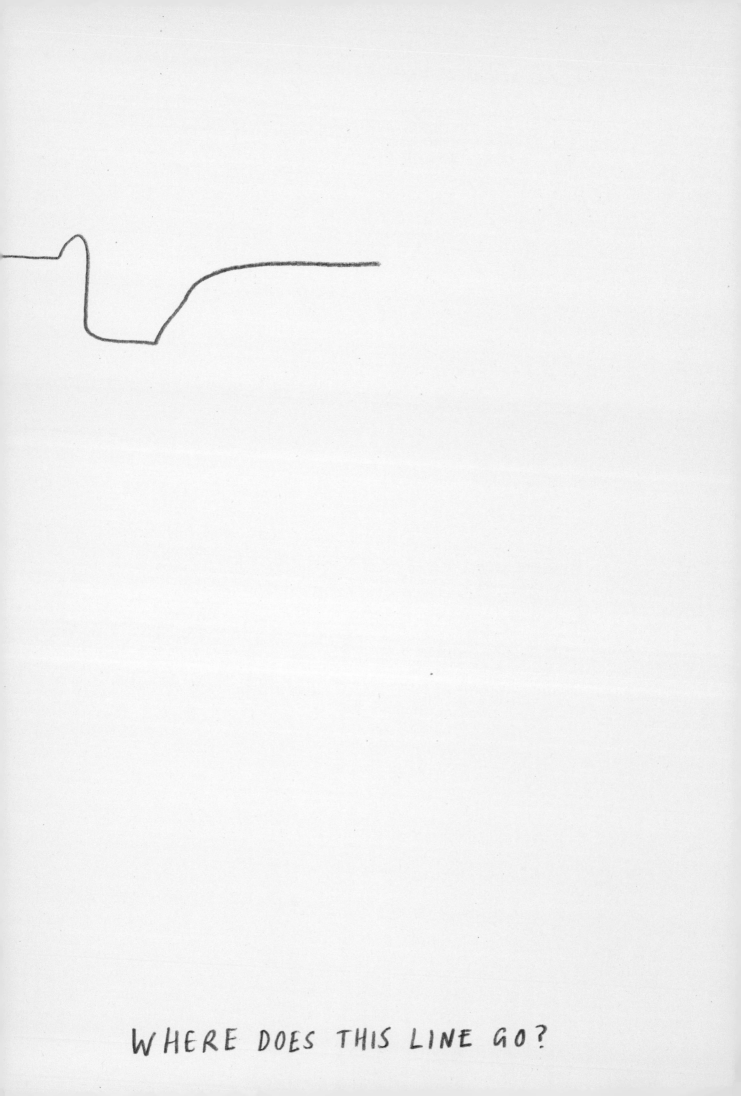

WHERE DOES THIS LINE GO?

A very big THANKYOU to:

Angus Hyland
for love and invaluable support.

Mark Cass. Cass Art
"LET'S FILL
THIS BOOK
WITH
ART"
produced for
CASS ART KIDS
was the
inspiration
for this book.
www.cassart.co.uk

Laurence King
Jo Lightfoot
Donald Dinwiddie
Felicity Awdry

thankyou for all
your support to
Darrel, Helen, Amanda,
Chloe and Jenny at
www.heartagency.com

Andrew Linge

Mrs Marion Deuchars (Snr)

www.mariondeuchars.com